FOLKLORE OF TRIBAL COMMUNITIES

FOLKLORE OF TRIBAL COMMUNITIES

ORAL LITERATURE OF THE SANTALS, KHARIAS, ORAONS AND THE MUNDAS OF ORISSA

By

Nityananda Patnaik

GYAN

Folklore of
Tribal Communities
(Oral Literature of the Santals, Kharias,
Oraons and the Mundas of Orissa)

ISBN : 978-81-212-0776-8

Published 2016 in India by
Gyan Publishing House
5, Ansari Road, Darya Ganj,
New Delhi - 110002
Phone : 9811692060

E-mail: books@gyanbooks.com
website: gyanbooks.com

Printed at : G. Print Process, Delhi

CONTENTS

ACKNOWLEDGEMENTS

The study on Folklore of nonliterate people is one of the important aspects of Anthropology. It consists of their myths, tales, proverbs, riddles and such other unwritten literary aspects of culture. This book presents a brief account of Oral literature of four tribal communities, namely the Santals, the Oraons, the Kharias, and the Mundas of Orissa. Most gratefully I acknowledge their depth of knowledge and experience in regard to their unwritten literary world.

I am also very much grateful to the Department of Culture under the Ministry of Human Resources Development, Government of India for providing financial assistance for documentation of this folk literature.

I wish to thankfully acknowledge the help extended to me by the investigating team of the institute for the fieldwork which they had undertaken to collect data about Oral Literature from the tribal communities.

I also thankfully express my gratitude to Mrs. Pratiti Mohanty for assembling the information collected by our investigators and drafting the preliminary report.

The Steno/Typists of the Social Science Development Research Institute (SSADRI) Mr. F. Samal and Mr. S. Patra sat down hours together typing out the report and bringing it to the final shape.

The computerization of the report and formatting for publication was done by Mr. Pradeep Satapathy of the Institute. It is his sincerity which brought the work to final shape.

I also thankfully express my gratitude to Mr. Durgacharan Panda, Artist who took pains in going through the work and made sketches accordingly.

Last but not the least I am very grateful to Mr. Amit Garg and Mr. B.P. Garg, Managing Director of the Gyan Publishing House for bringing out this book in time.

I sincerely hope that this modest attempt will help the folklorists and encourage them for further study of the folklore of the Tribes of Orissa which are vanishing with the passage of time.

Nityananda Patnaik

PREFACE

The present study is based upon the field work conducted on the Folklore of four different tribes of Orissa namely Santal, Kharia, Oraon and Munda in the two different districts.

Folklore is a medium through which the soul of the human being expresses itself colourfully and in such creation it finds an artistic fulfilment and entertainment. This is no less true in the case of these tribes of Orissa. Myths, legend and folklore all being parts of the same oral tradition, intertwine and influence each other. Themes from mythology sometimes occur in legends, while in simple cultures myths are hard to separate from folktales. Nevertheless, each of the three types does have a particular character of its own. Mythology is closely bound-up with religion. Its concern is with matters that shape the lives of men, the creation of the world, the origin of life and the meaning of death, etc. Myths are set in a distant and unrecognisable past. Legends on the other hand, have a known historical past. In legends facts are moulded in an imaginative or even fantastic way, their heroes often possessing magical or super natural powers. But they are rooted in reality. Folklore the third category of Oral tradition, includes songs and ballads, dances and music, *impromptu* drama and traditional customs and beliefs. All these are important in maintaining a culture.

In the present work within the limited space and obviously with a view to securing the appeal to a wider public, it has been possible for me just to present some of the collections of the folklores of the four different tribes, such as Santal, Kharia, Oraon and Munda from the two different districts of Orissa. The study concerns the Hill Kharias and the Santals of Mayurbhanj district and the Oraon and Munda of Sundergarh district. We have taken some of the folklores of these four tribes and described them with comparative fullness. We have also given in short an account regarding their general features, customs and institutions and observed certain important variations. These four different communities represent four different types and stages of primitive culture and thus furnish fruitful materials in the study of Social Anthropology for a comparative study and clear comprehension of the earlier stages in the evolution of human culture.

Nityananda Patnaik

INTRODUCTION

Since time immemorial man has accommodated himself well with the surroundings. Human ecology studies this interrelationship with the physical environment and the manner in which the habitat moulds the group, their manners and institutions. The physical conditions influence the distribution of population and determine the size of the localities, develop the eating habits, dress patterns, vocations and trades and the pattern of civilization and culture of the groups. This however is not the whole truth, the social aspects of man, his migratory habits and his ingenuity has enabled him to use, explore and exploit the natural phenomena around him to his best with consequent impact on his group. The cultural phases and technological change through which the social groups have passed explain the types of society that are developed and got extinct for the better that were evolved. The succession and the coexistence of the types of society such as the tribal, agrarian and post-industrial explains the phenomena of this change.

The simple people of the tribal communities are spread throughout the length and breadth of the country. The forest dwellers, the hillmen, the shifting cultivators, hunting and food gathering communities follow their respective life style, work habits and traditions. They are humble and contented. Their family ties are fostered by the age-old customs and they have a strong belief in an all powerful providence. Often, this faith of theirs in a superior being, manifests itself in their reverence for anything which appears to be peculiar be it a piece of stone, an animal, a river, a hill, a forest or even an idea.

Tribal people according to the ımperial Gazetteer is a collection of families bearing a common name, speaking a common dialect, occupying or professing to occupy a common territory and is not usually endogamous though originally it might have been so. The old tribalisation began simultaneously with the process of urbanization. The tribals have remained unassimilated due to their physical isolation in the inaccessible terrain.

Tribal societies are in most cases small in size. They possess a personality, religion and world view of their own, corresponding to their level of development. The tribes such as the Santals,

Gonds and Bhils are quite large numerically and developed considerably compared to hunting and food gathering communities.

Orissa: Land, People and It's Tribal Culture

Orissa occupies a unique position in the ethnographic map of India for having the largest variety of tribal communities.

Being one of the fascinating ethnographic states of the country it has been the homeland of many different tribal communities.

Orissa is situated between 17°49' N and 22°34' N latitudes and between 81°27' E and 87°29'E longitudes on the eastern coast of India. It is bounded by the states of West Bengal on the Northeast, Jharkhand on the North, Madhya Pradesh on the West, Andhra Pradesh on the South and the Bay of Bengal on the East. Its capital is located in the historic city of Bhubaneswar, the city of temples.

Orissa is unique in the country for its splendours, bounties of nature, panorama of social life and culture and glorious achievements of its people in art and architecture. Here is a State which is endowed with all that the people of all walks of life, artists, architects, anthropologists, historians, sociologists, pilgrims and tourists like to visit. The sea view, lake view, greenery of forest, hot springs, water falls, high hills, river gorges, are some of the gifts of the sprawling beauty of nature. Amidst such natural bounty are present wild life sanctuaries, zoological parks and botanical gardens which comprise some of the natural endowments of great attraction.

Apart from its distinctive land scape, Orissa is famous for ancient monuments, caves, monasteries and places of pilgrimage. The temples in the cathedral city of Bhubaneswar and Sun temple at Konark and the famous temple of Lord Jagannath at Puri, beckon people of different parts of country as well as international tourists to have a glimpse of such master-pieces of engineering skill and architecture; statues and paintings and arts and crafts of great craftsmen.

The marvels created by human hands are not only seen in the shane of richly sculptured temples and further ancient monuments but they are also reflected in many fine art such as tie and dye textiles, applique, *patta chitra*, terracotta, *dhokra* works turned out by lost wax process.

On the top of scenic beauty, temples and monuments, rock edicts and caves the tribes of Orissa are most fascinating and attract the scholars, academicians, artists, ethnographers and many other specialists of science of man. The 62 tribal communities that inhabit the state are widely different from one another in settlement patterns, house types, dress and ornaments, economic pursuits and social organizations, their fiestas and festivals, plastic and performing arts, dance and music and in language and folklore.

On one hand of the folk-urban spectrum there are hunting and food gathering Birhors, Bondos and Kharias, swidden cultivators like the Juangs, Lanjia Saoras and Kutia Kondhs, and at the other there are the Gonds, Santals, Oraons, Mundas and the Kisans who have taken to settled cultivation in plains and many of them live mostly as unskilled labourers in industrial and mining belts. In between these two extremes are found many tribal groups who are noted for their horticulture, handicraft and cattle breeding. Some of the tribal groups like the Santals, Oraons, Juangs and Gadabas are famous for their songs and dances which punctuate their individual and social life. Appropriate to different social and ritual occasions, different songs are sung and different dances are performed. To them dance and song are part of their life and source of enjoyment and relaxation. Different musical instruments are played in accompaniment of singing and dancing, on occasions of birth, marriage, name giving, attaining of puberty, sowing of seeds, harvesting, wearing new flowers and eating new fruits and new crops, hunting, thanks giving to the ancestral spirits-every occasion has its appropriate songs and dances.

FOLKLORE

The folklore of the tribals is the storehouse of oral literature which covers folk tales, myths, legends, folk songs, riddles, proverbs, folk speeches and stories. It also includes folk art of both graphic and plastic arts and folk dance.

The term folklore is defined by some scholars as the knowledge of a group of people. One of the traditional meaning of folklore indicates that it is an oral tradition. Folklore can be discussed and described under four major items. They are folk literature, folk arts including song and dance, folk beliefs and customs and folk crafts and languages. Folklore also reveals the aspirations, values and goals of people. The definitions taken together, explain how folklore helps in the oral exchange of knowledge in a non-literate society.

Folklore gives us clues to the hidden reactions to social sanctions that on the surface seem to be complied with willingly enough.

Folklore also creates a world where vindications that the world of reality denies, are granted and are to be found in stories wherein the weak prevail over the strong, where the evil meets an avenger or where many other of the less pleasant conditions of life are resolved in ways that are not those of work-a-day world. Some details about different components of folklore are briefly described below.

Folklore performs many functions. Myths explain the universe and provides a basis for rituals and beliefs. Tales are regarded as an unwritten record of tribal history. Proverbs garnish conversation with pointed allusion, help clarify an obscure reference to one deficient in worldliness and morality. Riddles help by serving as a test of wits. From legends people draw all ideas necessary to their existence.

Folklore reflects both its natural and cultural setting. From a great collection of myths are abstracted descriptions of tribe's material culture, economy, social structure, religious belief, life cycle, etc.

A folktale that incorporates details of an earlier period in the history of the people who tell it, documents that earlier life (living lore).

COMPONENTS OF FOLKLORE

Folk literature

The tribal folk literature is largely an artistic expression of tribal thought, emotions, feelings, happy moments of dancing, hunting, merry making, and also sorrowful memories connected with frustration, crop failure, distress and disappointments. In most cases it is available in spoken language and not in any written form. Every tribal community has its own language. For example, the Santal tribe speaks Santali belonging to Mundari language. The Santal tribe is an exceptional case as unlike many other tribal communities it has a script of its own which is called *Ol-Chiki*. Different items of folklore like folk literature, myths, legends, etc. are in written form, some written in Oriya script, some written in English script, but mostly in *Ol-Chiki*. The written versions are however not exhaustive. Many of the folklores are memorised in spoken language.

The folk literature is of many types such as (i) Folktale, (ii) Myth, (iii) Legend, (iv) Folk song, (v) Riddle, (vi) Proverb and (vii) Folk speech.

These types are in both prosaic and poetic forms. The folk tales, myths and legends are in prosaic order and in story form while the folk songs, riddles, proverbs are in the form of folk poetry.

Folk Tales

Folk tales are different from myths and legends although these three items bear the characters of a story such as a plot, incident, conflict, climax, motivation, and development of character. The distinguishing characters of folk tales are that the tales have their roots in the distant past, and depict the inner feelings and emotions.

The folk tales are composed of a mixture of actuality and fantasy. The folk tales can be classified into two categories such as (1) the tales having no poetic elements and (2) tales having poetic elements in the form of verses or proverbs.

Myths

Myths are an important part of the prose order of the folklore. A myth contains a plot on the faith of a tribal community concerning supernatural beings and imaginary persons or things. Myth is not legend as the former is not historically true and it is not also folktales as it centres round mythological characters, that is, spirits, gods and goddesses. Myth is the product of the intellectual thoughts of folk mind. Myths describe the origin of natural and cosmic bodies. Thus the myths can be classified into two categories such as 1. functional myths and 2. cosmogonic myths. The functional myths are related to every day life covering customs, behaviour, social activities such as food habits, dress, youth organization, dance etc. The cosmogonic myths are concerned with creation of universe, water, fire, sun, moon, stars, thunder, lightening and many other cosmic phenomena.

Legend

One character which distinguishes legend from folk tale and myth is that the legends are believed to be historically true. Legends refer to an exaggerated and colourful account of an event. According to many folklorists, the legends are considered traditional oral narratives which are regarded as true by the narrators and the members of the society in which such legends are circulated. But the historians do not attach any importance on the legends to substantiate any event in the history. The legends in general speak of persons, places, and events giving descriptions of heroic actions and some thing wonderful. There are also anecdotal legends describing something which reflects intelligence of persons and animals and things of amusing character.

Riddles

W.H. Jansen has defined the riddles as "A riddle is a question, direct or indirect, complete or incomplete, in traditional form, whereby the questioner challenges a listener to recognize and identify the accuracy, the unit, the truth in a statement that usually seems implausible or self-contradictory, but that is true in its own peculiar light.

In other words, a riddle is a witty and puzzling question related to something which is obscure. The questioner asks this question asking the listeners to say what that thing is.

The riddles may be broadly classified into two types namely riddles of structure dichotomous found in the proportions and riddles of description (obscure in nature). The riddles of structure may be divided into two categories namely 1. riddles containing one self-contradictory proposition and 2. riddles containing more than one self-contradictory propositions in sequential order.

Proverbs

According to R.B. Browne, "To the most credulous members of society proverbs and the proverbial expressions are the accumulated knowledge of the ages, the voice of the history, they are tried and true, and as such are pragmatic unassailable wisdom". According to Archer Tylor and B.J. Whiting the description of proverbs as "short, plain, common, figurative, ancient and true", is as good as any formal definition. They have also characterized the proverbs as "Sayings" which "summaeses" a situation and in its own inimitable way passes some sort of judgement on it or characterizes the essence". Proverb in a large measure is thought to be the wisdom of many and wit of one.

Folk speech

Folk speeches are the everyday spoken language of the people. These speeches are used on certain special occasions. Such items as teasing, joking, taunting, cursing, blessing, chanting, oath taking, insulting and sarcastically speaking, are some of the expressions which come under the folk speeches of folklore. Similarly gestures, greetings, bidding farewell, nicknaming, etc. are also the folk speeches.

Folk Art

Artistic performances are part of folklore. Both graphic and plastic arts are covered under folk art. Some of the art types are : (i) carving and engraving, (ii) clay figures, (iii) painting, (iv) weaving patterns, (v) tattooing, (vi) ornamentation.

Carving and Engraving

The designs of carving and engraving are found on wooden pillars, roof rafters, tobacco containers, combs, etc. These are of the types of chevron and zigzag lines, folding and ball shaped carved designs and hatching and carved figures of human beings, birds and animals, boundary lines with triangle shaped designs engraved along the lines, floral and lozenge designs.

Clay Modeling

Sculpturing and clay modeling are found among the tribal communities. In size these are very small and of various types.

Painting

Some tribal communities like the Santals and Saoras are noted for wall paintings, the former doing it with a decorative motive and the latter for ritual and magical purposes. Mostly coloured earth is used in wall paintings, line drawings, human and animal figures, floral and various types of geometric designs and different types of objects and activities which catch the imagination of the painters who are invariably women among the Santals and Sorcerers among the Saoras, A typical Santal house, its floor, walls, pillars and doors is given a colour wash in coloured earth (black, gray, red, yellow and white) with designs of various types drawn on them.

Weaving

The tribal communities make mats by weaving leaves of date palm. The point to be noted in mat making is what patterns are followed in weaving. The patterns which are generally observed are check and twilled patterns. In basket making these patterns are also used, but the materials used in basketry are bamboo splits or *Siali* barks. Some tribal communities do the weaving of cloths by means of their indigenous handlooms. Some use cotton yarn and the primitive sections use bark strands for weaving the cloths which they wear. In fencing poles are stuck upright into the ground and tough twigs are twined onto the poles.

Tattooing

The tribal communities do the tattooing on their body. Generally the arms and breasts are tattooed. Certain section of the Kondh tribe do the tattooing on their face. Lines, dots, floral designs are generally tattooed on the body.

Folk Song and Folk Dance

Some of the primitive sections of the tribal groups like the Bondos and Dongrias, Juangs and Saoras, Gadabas and Parajas are most colourful and are frequented by tourists and visitors. Whatever may be their economic backwardness and development most tribal communities have a fairly high level of performing and plastic arts. Songs and dances punctuate their individual and social life. Appropriate to different social and ritual occasions different songs are sung and different dances are performed. To them dances and songs are part of their life and source of enjoyment and relaxation. Different musical instruments (*Nagara*, *Tamak*, *Dholki*, Flute, Cymbol, Gong, String instruments) are used in accompaniment of singing and dancing. Birth, death, marriage, name giving, attainment of puberty sowing of seeds, harvesting, wearing new flowers and eating new crops and fruits, hunting, curing illness, thanksgiving to dead ancestors and unseen spirits and Gods-every occasion has its appropriate songs and dances.

Their song-poems are charged with livid intensity. Often passionate experiences speak simply, quietly and without any concern to decorate or beautify their thoughts and feelings. Their theme is universal and timeless like the meandering hill-streams and never divorced from basic human concern. They express emotions concretely, unobtrusively. Whether it is the Juang love song, the Paraja marriage song, the Santal *Bakhen*, or the Kondh *Meriah* song-the qualities mentioned above stand out in clear outlines, unmistakable and moving in their intensity.

Although there are several characteristic features common to different tribal groups, every tribe has its unique pattern of dance. A few examples are given to illustrate tribe wise distinctiveness in dance.

The most celebrated Koya dance features a long row of girls with heavy ornaments and caps on their heads. They dance by striking a rhythm which is produced by hitting the ground with sticks fitted with bells. They dance and sing forming a series of winding and unwinding circles to the tune of the music provided by the male members who put on the spectacular headgear fitted with bison-horns with strings of *cowries* hanging in front. This is the tribe which uses the longest double membrane drums.

Among the Paraja, the most characteristic dance is known as '*Demsa*'. Girls who put on typical short sarees and deck their heads with flowers form a long row by interlocking their arms. They move with typical swinging motion in a graceful formation. The girl who leads the dance holds a bunch of peacock feathers by which she gives direction of their movements. The dance starts with a stylized walk in slow tempo ending in a fast moving climax. The music is provided by the male members.

The Gadaba dance does not differ much from that of the Paraja except in their dress and characteristic ornaments. The girls put on *keranga* cloth and large coils of metal wares in their ear-lobes almost touching the shoulders and do their unique hair-style. The music is again provided by the male members.

The Kondh girls in their special attire and inter-locking arms dance to the music played on by the male members. The movement of the group is sometimes forward and backward and on other occasion coiling and uncoiling circles.

In case of the Saoras, persons belonging to all age grades irrespective of sexes join the dance. The dancers hold sticks, umbrellas, axes and other similar objects and move forward and backward to the accompanying music.

Among the Bhuinyas and the Juangs of North Orissa, the popular dance is called *changu* dance. Boys standing in a row sing and beat changu (a single membrane drum) and the girls interlocking their arms dance in front of them by moving forward and backward. The most striking feature of their dance is the musical sound produced by the girls by hitting their metal bangles against each other.

Among the Santals, both boys and girls dance with interlocking arms and in long rows. The dance is to the music played by the male members. The most important features of their dance are the movements of feet, arms and the head. The Oraon dance too resembles the Santal dance. In both these cases the musical orchestra is provided by the male members. The section which follows gives a few examples of songs and dances and prayers particularly of the Santals who are noted for literary excellence.

The Santals

Ethnographic Account

Identification, Origin and History

Thee forest clad, undulated and hilly regions of the district of Mayurbhanj and its adjoining areas of Keonjhar and Balasore districts are inhabited by many Mundari speaking tribes, amongst whom the most predominating community is the Santal. Numerically speaking this community is one of the largest tribes of Orissa. The district of Mayurbhanj claims 76.01 per cent of the total Santal population of the state. Next to this district comes Balasore followed by Keonjhar district which had 11.20 per cent and 7.76 per cent respectively of the total Santal population.

The Santal of Orissa never claim their present habitat as their original homeland. Rather they are proud of describing a legend which tells "*Ahiri pipiri*" as their birth place and "*Chaichampa*" as their fort located somewhere in Bihar. In the past, the Santals were of nomadic habit and used to wander from place to place in quest of agricultural land. Some scholars link up their traditional homeland to central India. Later on they came to Chotanagpur plateau and the adjoining districts of Midnapur and Singhbhum. In the end of 18th century they made their home in Santal Pragana. At present they are spread over a large tract of land within the geographical jurisdiction of West Bengal, Bihar, Orissa, Assam and Tripura. They constitute one of the largest tribes in the country as a whole. Most of the Santal settlements are more or less permanent in nature. Sometimes individual families shift their house sites when there is scarcity of land around the settlements to feed their growing population.

The Santal speak a language known as Santali which belongs to Munda group of Astro-Asiatic sub-family of the

Austric family. At present most of them can speak and understand Oriya.

Nature of Settlement

A Santal village comprises a number of households surrounded by agricultural fields and pastures. The villages are big, the average size varying from 50 to 100 households. The villages are lineally arranged on either side of the road. Adjacent to each village there must be one common sacred grove '*Jaher*', consisting of Sal, Asan, Nim trees in which their village deities reside, '*Manjhi-than*', another ritual spot of the village is

located in front of the house of the *Manjhi*, the secular headman of the village. *Manjhi-than* is the seat of the spirit of the founder headman of the village.

Household Furniture and Articles

The Santal house may be one-roomed or a cluster of several rooms constructed according to the needs of the family. The household articles of the Santals no more constitute their traditional materials like earthen pots, leaf cups and plates etc. On the other hand there are greater inflow of modern articles like aluminium and brass utensils, cooking pots, radio, cycle, watch, etc. Their other household materials consist of some agricultural, hunting and fishing tools, musical instruments, baskets, broom sticks, string cots etc., which they make themselves or get them by exchanging agricultural products.

Dress and Personal Adornment

The typical way of dressing of the Santals distinguishes them from the local non-tribals. The men wear rough *Dhoti* or *Gamchha* and women wear green, blue check print sarees woven by local weavers. Now a days mill-made clothes are also used. The use of petticoats, blouses have become a common fashion for young women.

In course of their close association with the local non-tribals, the Santal women seem to have changed their taste of using ornaments. To have tattoo mark on the arm of the male members is an universal practice among the Santals. But no ritual importance is attached to it. Again for the Santal women tattooing is a common fashion, and they make tattoo marks of various designs on arms, wrists and chests.

Food

Rice is the staple food of the Santals all the year round. Their staple food is substituted by other cereals such as minor millets and wheat and vegetables and dry-fish and pulses are taken as side dishes. The Santals relish various fruits available in the area. The main fruits are mango and jackfruit which are eaten both at the green and ripe stage. When they catch fish from agricultural field or other water sources like river, pond or canal they get chance of enjoying fish and dry fish. The domestic animals like goats, pigs are generally slaughtered on festive occasions for feast. Rice beer called *handia* continues to be the traditional drink, and is taken when old friends, relatives get together at festivals and funerals, at birth, marriages and betrothals, *handia* is also offered to their ancestral spirits on ceremonial occasions and also when it is brewed at home before anybody drinks it.

Birth

During pregnancy a woman observes various taboos and restrictions to protect herself and her baby in her womb from all evil spirits. As a protection against ghosts, spirits and witches she is not allowed to go alone to the forest, to touch corpse or to go to cremation grounds. She does all sorts of household work, but avoids hard manual labour.

When labour pain starts the expectant mother is kept confined in a separate room to which male members are not allowed to enter. A traditional midwife called Mukhi assists her in delivering the child. After birth the midwife cuts the umbilical cord, bathes the child and mother and puts the placenta, etc., in a pit in the same room. The mother is considered ritually unclean. She remains secluded till the purificatory rites are performed. The ceremony takes place on the 7th or 9th day of child birth. On this day all family members take a purificatory bath, wash their clothes and houses and used earthen pots are thrown away.

The name giving ceremony takes place on any day within one year. The relatives and the village elders are invited on the occasion. When all assemble, the midwife brings the child and selects a name from among the dead ancestors either of paternal or maternal side.

Marriage

Puberty marks the beginning of a full-fledged womanhood. When a girl attains puberty she is not allowed to enter into cowshed or *Bhitar*, the Sacred place of the house. When the period is over she takes a full bath.

The most significant and turning point in the life of an individual is the marriage. Marriage makes an individual a full-fledged member of the community. From economic point of view a man gets a life partner who can help him in economic pursuits. They have definite rules and regulations of marriage. Main restrictions on marriage are tribal endogamy, clan exogamy and exclusion of cross-cousin marriage. Of all forms of marriages the most frequent are marriage by negotiation and Diku marriage. Negotiations are first initiated by the boy's party. The elders of both parties exchange several visits and on such occasions fixation of bride-price forms one of the most common points of discussion. Bride price is paid both in cash and kind consisting of a few rupees, cow, bullock etc., If both parties approve the proposal, a day is fixed for marriage. On the wedding day the bride with a party arrives at the boy's place where marriage ceremony is held.

Widow remarriage is permitted in Santal society and she is allowed to marry her husband's younger brother. Divorce is socially permitted and is initiated either by husband or wife. If a woman leaves her husband and elopes with another man, the second husband would return the marriage expenses and bride price.

Death

The Santals ascribe various reasons such as natural causes, supernatural agencies, witchcraft for their sufferings. For sickness they first refer to '*Ojha*', the village medicine man-cum spirit doctor. The *Ojha* either prescribes herbal medicine or applies magico-religious methods to detect the cause of disease. Any type of chronic or serious disease is believed to be the evil effect of spirit.

Just like birth and marriage, death also involves many rituals. The Santals believe that the spirit of the dead remains in the house and may cause harm to the family members and the villagers in general till the death rituals are performed. So they hasten to perform obsequies as early as possible, within 5 to 20 days after the death. The first purificatory ritual is observed when all the male members of the lineage group shave their head and women pare their nails and smear turmeric paste on their body. All take bath. On this occasion various rites and rituals are performed and the spirit of the dead is offered food.

The Santals believe in ceremonial immersions of bone of the deceased in a holy river which is called *Damodar Jatra* after the name of the river Damodar. The Santals now living in different localities have different *ghat* in the nearby river where the last death ritual is performed and the bone of the deceased is immersed.

Social Organisation and the Regulation of Santals

The Santal tribe is divided into a number of clans known as *Paris*. The clans are unilateral descent groups whose members trace their origin to some common mythical ancestor.

Usually each of these clans is named after some natural phenomena, animals or any other object. *Hansda* means (duck). *Marandi* is a kind of weed. People of *Hansda* clan do not eat duck or its eggs. Those belonging to *Murmu* clan do not kill cow. The members of a clan are considered brothers and sisters and as such marriage or sexual relations among them is a taboo. Each clan is again divided into a number of sub-clans and marriage is prohibited among the sub-clan members. Those who disobey this rule are generally excommunicated. For them severe punishment is imposed by the hunt council which is the traditional supreme court of the tribe. Each sub-clan is again divided into a number families who are of one lineage group *(bansa)*. The *Bansa* members offer certain sacrifices at definite occasions to the *Abge Bonga*. The lineage members have greater sense of solidarity. They do not have any specific term for the lineage group. They refer it as *Kutumba*, an Oriya term used to designate the lineage members. They are called on to attend the death, birth and marriage ceremonies. A close kinship tie and greater co-operation among the lineage members are observed.

Family, the smallest social unit among them is patrilineal, patrilocal and patripotestal. Descent is reckoned through father's line. According to their residential pattern a girl after her marriage leaves her father's house and lives in her husband's place. Most of the Santal families are nuclear, comprising husband, wife and unmarried children and sometimes grand parents. The sons after they are married are separated and live in their respective houses and enjoy their respective share of their parents' property. Authority is vested on the eldest male member of the household.

Political Organisation

The smallest unit of the traditional political organisation is the village council. It is composed of office bearers and the village elders. The council is headed by a *Manjhi* or Headman, who is assisted by the *Paramanik* or the assistant headman, the *Naik*, the village priest, *Jog Manjhi* or the moral guardian of the village youth. The meeting of the council generally takes place at the *Manjhi Than*.

The village council is the important social unit for administration of justice. Family and village disputes are referred to the council. They have their traditional village Panchayat which settles their socio-religious problems. Due to introduction of statutory Panchayat the old system is fading away.

Religious Practices and Belief System

The Santals have well-knit religious organisation. They believe in various deities, ghosts and spirits residing in hills, forests and streams and the ancestral spirits guiding their every walk of life. *Thakur* or *Sing Bonga* or *Dharam* is their supreme deity who is identified with the Sun and is worshipped with great reverence. He is the creator of the universe and a benevolent deity. There is no specific festival to worship 'Him' but in every important festival, He is remembered. Their village deities are *Maran Buru*, *Mareko*, *Turuiki*, *Jaher Era*, *Gosae Era* who reside in the village Jahera (a patch of a holy grove located at the outskirt of the village). The village deities play a vital role in the life of the Santals and control their socio-economic activities. Another important deity or spirit is *Manjhi Haram* Bonga who resides in the *Manjhi-than* which is located in the village in front of the house of the village headman or *Manjhi*. *Manjhi Bonga* is the spirit of the founder of the village. In addition to these, they worship *Abge Bonga* or household spirits, *Buru Bonga* (hill deities), *Rango Bonga* (forest deities) and *Basumata* or mother earth. In order to keep them in good temper the Santals observe a number of festivals spread over different months of the year. Most important of their festivals are *Erok-sim*, *Harihar-sim*, *Iri-Guldi-sim*, *Janthal*, *Saharas*, *Magha-sim* and *Baha* which are associated with agricultural operations. *Erok sim* marks the beginning of sowing the seeds in the fields. *Harihar-sim* is observed for the offering of first millet crop. *Janthal* is a celebration of the first fruit of the winter rice crops. *Magh-sim* is observed in the month of *Magha*, which marks the end of the year. During *Baha* festivals the Santals offer the first fruit of *Mahua*, wild flowers and fruits to the *Jaher* deities.

Bonga worship is mainly done out of fear. They have strong belief in their own religion. Now a days however they have also started worshipping local Hindu gods and goddesses.

The social and religious life of the Santals who live in the villages have been least affected by the outside forces. They follow their traditional customs and manners in respect of death, birth and marriage ceremonies. The Santals observe various rites and rituals to avoid displeasure of the Bongas. However some local Hindu gods and goddesses have entered into Santal pantheon.

Economic Life

The main occupation of the Santals is settled agriculture. In recent times both men and women are engaged in cultivation. Emergence of mining and industrial establishments both in and outside home district have provided them scope for occupational mobility. The economic activities in the Santal community are carried out with the cooperation and participation of both sexes. However agriculture which is the mainstay of the Santal does not provide adequate means for their maintenance round the year. They supplement it by forest collection and wage earning through manual labour. When the harvesting season is over, they generally migrate to towns and industrial belts to earn daily wages. The landless Santals during agricultural season are employed as agricultural labourers in the same locality. With the passage of time they have passed the stage of food gathering and hunting and have become cultivators and agricultural labourers. The country which was once covered under thick forest has become almost bare of vegetation. Even though wild animals have become rare, the habit of hunting has become merely a kind of ritual.

The last day of *Baha* festival marks the beginning of the communal hunting. Elaborate rituals are followed before the actual hunting begins. Success in hunting indicates good luck for them ensuring a bumper crop for the year. Besides they hunt birds by using bow and arrow when they are free from work.

Fishing does not form an important source of income for the Santals, but it supplies a delicious menu to their diet. The fishing appliances used by them constitute nets and traps in rainy season, and the agriculture fields become the fishing ground and all who have land catch fish with the help of basket trap. The Santals keep cows, bullocks, goats, sheep, poultry and pigs for domestic consumption and sale.

The weekly market called *hat* plays an important role in Santal economy. Except those, who live in close proximity of towns, others mostly depend on local *hat* for purchase of their daily necessities and sale of agricultural and forest produces. Now LAMPS and TDCC centres have been established in the Santal area to provide article of daily consumption and for disposing of surplus agricultural produce and surplus forest produce at a responsible rate.

The Santals have experienced different socio-economic

changes in recent times. They live amidst various castes and tribes. The influence of Hindu neighbours can be seen in some aspects of their culture. Urbanization and industrialization and interaction with the Hindus have changed the outlook of the Santals to a great extent. Large number of Santals go out in search of job and work in towns and urban centres, where from they come back with new ideas and practices.

Like other tribes of Orissa the Santals are fond of dance and music. They dance and sing when they are in happy mood. Dance and music are associated with all the rituals and festivals. This is a way to get pleasure and relaxation from daily routine of work. The Santal dance is a group affair. Boys and girls, old and young participate in dance. There is no hard and fast rule regarding the time and place for dancing. But they generally dance at night. The dancers do not wear any special dress during performances. The main musical instruments used by the Santals are *Tamak*, *Dhol*, *Bhuang*, *Sarangi* and flutes.

They have different types of songs for different occasions. Their devotional songs are sung during religious ceremonies.

The Santal women show their artistic talents while decorating their walls with different colours and drawings. Their houses are most picturesque among the tribes of Orissa.

FOLKLORES OF THE SANTALS

From the very dawn of human society, man has tried to explain the mysteries of creation and life by means of stories. This is true both of the so called civilized and unlettered folks who sought thereby to throw some light on inexplicable phenomena by weaving tales round them to satisfy the hunger for knowledge. Here instead of tracing the origin of myths and legends, we wish to introduce to the reader the wealth of Santal folklore with the idea that it might illuminate the dim recesses of the Santal mind, and show how they think and feel in the presence of the baffling mysteries of life and how they interpret them. The old *Manjhi* of the Santal village like the grandmother is the repository of these tales. Men, old and young gather round him in moments of leisure and listen to him with rapt attention as he tells stories seasoning them with flashes of humour, propounding riddles to the listeners and by adorning the stories with morals as the experience of her ripe old age.

In the following discussion we will give the readers a collection of Santal folklore as gathered from Mayurbhanj.

STORIES

KAHU AR TUYU (Crow and Jackal)

Once a crow brought a piece of meat by its beak and sat over the branch of a Kusum tree which was seen by a Jackal and he followed the crow. The Jackal thought to snatch the meat from the crow for which he approached the crow. The Jackal initiated conversation with the crow saying "crow brother; I have been looking for you for the last few days, but could not meet you. I am eager to listen to your song and please sing a song".

The crow being exhilarated started singing loudly opening his beak. The moment he opened his beak, the meat fell down. The Jackal immediately grabbed it and ran away. The crow followed him, but the Jackal went into his den. The crow was cheated and bore the loss while the clever Jackal won over the crow.

TUYU AR BHENDE (Jackal and Sheep)

Once upon a time a Jackal went to a village to catch a hen. He looked for the hen at one end of the village, but the dogs of the village saw him and chased him to a very long distance. Being afraid of the dogs the Jackal jumped into a well. At that time a sheep was passing by that well. The Jackal called the sheep from the well to rescue him and the sheep being unable to bear the condition of the jackal jumped into the well to save him. After entering the well the sheep advised the jackal to get out of the well by mounting on his back. Accordingly the Jackal followed the instructions and came out of the well, but the Jackal did not bother to rescue the sheep from the well and as a result the sheep died in the well.

BIRODHI BHEDA (Birodhi sheep)

In a village there were two sheep who often used to fight with each other. Whoever would see them fight they would send them in different ways. Their owner also had to send them to graze at separate places. But once both the sheep came face to face with each other, they both rushed immediately after seeing each other and banged their heads against the wall situated at the middle of a bridge. As a result their skulls cracked and they died at the spot. The lesson learnt is that it is no good being antagonistic to anyone.

HATI AR SAKAN CHENE (Elephant and the leaf bird)

In a forest there was an elephant who was very notorious and was wild in character. In that forest, in a Sal tree, two leaf birds were living and had also given birth to several baby birds. Once the notorious elephant went and rubbed his body against the Sal tree. The tree was not very big and so it started shaking to and fro. The birds requested him not to do so as there were baby birds which might fall out of the nest. The elephant did not bother about them. So the birds got furious and threatened the elephant to stop or else face the consequences. The elephant replied saying, they may do anything they want. So hearing this both the birds entered into his ears and started chirping inside. Then the elephant helplessly ran away leaving the place and requested them to leave him alone asking for forgiveness. From that day the elephant never troubled anyone.

Thus we can conclude that the forest dwellers as the Santals are, have folk-tales attributing human traits to animals. The lessons of these stories are sometimes quite clear, and it is more interesting to see how animal life has been interpreted by the forest dwellers.

The Wicked Jackal

A mother and son were living in a village. The name of the son was Anup. He did ploughing everyday and did not return home to have his food. Therefore his mother used to take his food to the field where he worked. A jackal saw her carrying food everyday for her son. The jackal approached her and asked her to give the food to him and said that he would create trouble otherwise. Being afraid of the Jackal she put the container on the ground and the Jackal ate up most of the food and left a small amount in the container for her son. This was an everyday affair and the son was underfed everyday. One day he asked his mother why she was bringing insufficient food for him. His mother narrated what the matter was.

In order to teach a lesson to the wicked jackal he asked his mother to do the ploughing and he would go himself to fetch the food. He wore the dress of an animal and appeared to be a woman. While walking down to his field he was held up by the jackal on the way and asked him to give him the food he was carrying. Anup put down the container on the ground and thereafter the jackal started eating the food. While he was busy eating Anup gave a beating to the jackal. The jackal ran away in terror leaving the food on the ground.

The jackal wanted to take revenge against the boy. He passed stool on his plough. But Anup also thought of doing some injury to the Jackal. He set a sharp razor and tied it to the plough handle on which the jackal was passing stool. Next time when the jackal was committing this nuisanse and rubbed his back he got a cutting injury on his buttock.

The jackal got angry and planned to do some harm to Anup. According to the plan the Jackal tried to destroy the bean plants which Anup grew in his field, but the jackal failed in his attempt because Anup put some thorny plants here and there in his field. The jackal scolded Anup and threatened him to eat up all his fowls.

The next day Anup took a sickle and sat down near the fowl pen. At night the jackal came and went straight to the fowl pen. When he was trying to catch some fowl Anup suddenly appeared before him and told him that he would cut down his neck. The jackal ran away in terror. The jackal cursed him that he would meet death soon.

Thereupon, Anup pretended to die, and his old mother went to the forest and cried before the jackal. The jackal appeared before her and asked "......When are you going to have the funeral ceremony ?" "Today" the old woman replied and invited the jackal to eat food in her house. The jackal accepted her request. In the evening the jackal came to her house along with a number of other jackals. After all of them were seated, the old woman pretended to cry. She then brought some cooking pots and kept them down. Then she lit a fire. The jackal then said, "old woman, tie us up for the present, otherwise we might fight with one another". The old woman tied them all up with a rope. The wicked jackal was also tied up firmly.

The old woman went to prepare food for the jackals. She pretended to cook by putting a pan on the fire. The wicked jackal jumped in joy when he heard the hissing sound coming from the pan.

In the meantime, Anup who had been lying down in his bhitar, came out to beat the jackal with a stick. All the jackals tore the rope and ran away except the wicked jackal who could not untie the rope. He was beaten until he fainted.

The following day the jackal was taken and tied to a post near the place where the people went to fetch water. A club was kept there. Every one who came to fetch water, gave him a beating with the club. As a result the body of the jackal swelled up.

Other jackals who passed by that place saw the condition of the wicked jackal and wanted to know as to how he became so fat. The jackal replied that he was being fed rice by the people who came to fetch water and therefore he became fat. One of them enquired whether they would be given food if they were tied up like him. The wicked jackal replied in the affirmative. But to make them believe he suggested that they untie him and get themselves tied up with the rope and wait till the next morning when people would come with food.

When it dawned next day, the other jackals who were tied up in place of the wicked jackal were delighted to see five women coming towards them. The women put their water-pots down and took the club and beat them. Then three or four women came and joined them. All of them beat them mercilessly to death. In this way that wicked jackal escaped safely and other jackals met death.

Sari

Sari was the only sister of her seven brothers. She stayed home. Her brothers went to the forest for hunting. One day her eldest brother had a flower fixed in his ears while returning home from the forest. On reaching the house he asked his sister to give him some water to drink. After drinking water the eldest brother asked her to scratch his head which was itching severely. Sari started scratching his head and saw the flower tucked in the hair near his ear. Her brother told her the place from where he got the flower. Knowing Sari requested him to take her to that place so that she would get some flowers.

One day the brother took her to that place. She plucked some flowers from the tree and kept them in a packet. Later she arranged the flowers in a garland. While doing so she got thirsty and sent her brother to get some water. The brother asked the Chameleon which was present in the tree to watch his sister.

After that the brother went to some unknown stream to fetch water. During that time, there was the wedding of a prince. The bridegroom's companions who were going on that road, took rest under the same tree. Music was being played. A man of Dama caste who was beating drums, was occasionally looking at the tree and found the little girl sitting in the tree. The Dama drummer informed about the girl to the king who was searching for a daughter-in-law. The king looked at the girl-a very beautiful girl he had ever seen. The people, then went up the tree and brought the girl down and made her sit in palanquin. Sari had no option but to sit in it. She told the Chameleon to inform her brother that she has been carried away by the king. While she was carried away in the palanquin she threw mustard seeds on the way to indicate the path in which she has been carried away. Not finding his sister the brother went on searching for her.

On the way he met with some goat herding boys. He asked them if they had seen the king's bridegroom party going that way. The boys replied that the party had gone this way long back. The brother proceeded further crying and searching for his sister.

On the way he met with a group of horse tending boys and asked them if they have found the bridegroom's party passing by. They replied that they saw the party long back. The brother went on and with the hope to get his sister. Finally Sari heard the cry of her brother and told the party that her brother must be somewhere nearby. But the king did not pay any heed to her request of getting her brother. The brother ran and reached the party and caught hold of his sister's hand. He sprinkled the water which he was carrying over the party. As a result the prince became a "Dama" man and the band party turned into foxes, wolves and other animals. The animals fled into the forest and the sister married the Dama boy and with her brother all returned home in a happy mood.

SANTAL LEGENDS

Virsikha

There are three burnt marks on the left hand of each and every Santal. According to them, these three marks signify life, death and rebirth. Once upon a time there lived a lady demon in the Santal society, who used to torture them very much. The people were looking for ways to kill her. There was a courageous Santal named Kherwal who had been fighting against this demon for years together. But gradually time passed away and he died and was born again and killed the demon. The people were pleased and were very proud of him. In order to remember Kherwal for all time to come, the Santals suggested something but Kherwal denied this proposal. He said, he was killed by an enemy and brought prosperity and good fortune for the whole community, so if people really want to remember him, then they should put three burnt marks on the left hand which will remain as a mark of remembrance of him. This mark will be named as *'Virshikha'*.

From this day onwards whenever a child takes birth in Santal family they make three burnt marks on the left hand of the infant with a heated iron rod which denotes life, death and rebirth. The three aspects according to their language are, 'Janam-Gaj-Janam', (Life-death-Life).

The name of Kherwal's wife was Kajal. To remember Kajal, all the Santal wives give tattoo marks on their body in black colour. In Santal language, it is called *'Kajal'*. This legend depicts their bravery.

Worship of the Sal Plant

Jaher-Era is the supreme goddess of the Santals, who is considered most powerful and almighty. She is so powerful that the Santals believe that her arrow can pierce into a rock. The first flowers and fruits are usually offered to the goddess and so also the domestic animals. Among the fruits and flowers mangoes and *mahua* are the important ones which are commonly offered. The first fruits and flowers are offered to *Jaher-Era* on the occasion of *Baha Bonga*. In each Santal village there is a sacred-grove which is called *Jahera* where there must be Sal trees. People consider *Jaher-Era* as the almighty and they expect that they will worship and make offerings to this goddess so that she will help them in many ways. There is a myth regarding the *Jaher-Era*. Once a Muslim tried to steal away this Goddess. But he failed in his attempt as *Majhis'* wife obstructed him while taking away the Goddess. Her arrow which was aimed at the thief struck the Sal tree and since then the tree is worshipped.

In the days gone by the Santals wanted to decide where to live and what to do for their livelihood. For this they had meetings and gatherings at different places i.e. under *Kendu* tree (Tiril) where, they were unsuccessful and they call it 'Leper-Tiril'. (Rotten diaspyres melanoxylon). Then they had meeting under the *Mahua* tree where again it was unsuccessful, which in their language is called '*Khade Matkam*'. Then they went to the Banyan tree '*Peterbale*'. Finally they gathered under a Sal tree where they succeeded and took a decision. So this is called '*Sari Sarjam*' which means sal, and they have been worshipping this tree.

The above legends symbolize the psychology of the people about gods and goddesses. They are great believers of their affinity with flora of their habitat and the gods living therein. They fear them and therefore rituals have become a part of their day to day life.

Hen Sacrifice

The practice of animal sacrifice occupies a prominent role in the matter of worshipping the Gods and Goddesses. The hen sacrifice is one of the most important features in all rituals. While sacrificing hen usually the neck is twisted and separated from the body. But the neck of the hen is not totally cut away or separated from the body while it is sacrificed to appease *Jaher-Era*.

In fact *Jaher-Era*, who is the Supreme Goddess of the Santals, is not really present at *Jaher*, that is, the sacred grove. It was stolen away by the Muslims who carried it over to 'Macca' and installed it there. Here when hen is sacrificed its neck is not totally cut but its neck is half cut in the same way as the Muslims do in their offering.

One Sided Thatching of the Jaher-Era Roof

Earlier, *Jaher-Era* was being worshipped only by the Santal women. But gradually male members have also started worshipping. It is usually a practice that the females thatch the roof of *Jahera* and as they are not allowed to climb on the roof, they thatch only one side of the roof. This practice continues even now.

Bride-Price

In a Santal family there lived two orphan brothers and sisters with their grand father. Farming was their main source of livelihood. The agricultural lands were usually found in the hilly regions. It was the summer season and the rainy season was over, making the land fertile for ploughing. One day their grand father went to the land with the plough to till the land. While assembling the parts he found that one of the nails of the plough was missing. He searched for it all around but in vain. He came back home searching for the same. When he was searching for the nail a tiger was watching him. So after a while the tiger asked the old man what he was searching. In reply the old man stated that he had lost a nail of the plough which he is searching. The tiger enquired of him that if he would search the same for the old man what would the old man give in return. The old man immediately retorted back that he would get his grand daughter married to the tiger if he could find the nail out for him. The tiger was delighted with the old man's reply and started searching for the nail. But the nail was stuck inside the plough which fell down when the old man descended the plough from his shoulder. The tiger saw the same and handed it over to the old man by picking it up from the ground. After receiving the nail the old man told the tiger that his grand daughter would come in a short while bringing his food. When he would send her back to fetch some water for him the tiger can kidnap her from the place.

After a while the grand daughter came with the lunch for the old man and was sent by him to fetch water. The girl then went immeditately to get water from the water-fall. In the meantime the girl's brother was hunting in the forest with a bow and arrow. While hunting he reached near the spring. A crane was sitting nearby which was aimed at by him. But the arrow missed its target and pierced into the left eye of the tiger and the tiger fell down and died at the spot. The girl along with her brother came back after fetching water. Seeing the girl the old man was astonished. The brother explained the whole story of killing the tiger. The old man also explained about his contract with the tiger. Hearing this the girl became enraged and cautioned the old man that she would not give any gift to him at the time of her marriage. As her mother had given birth to her, so she would get *palat* i.e. a kind of cloth at her marriage. Her grand father would not get anything whether or not he is alive or dead by that time. He would receive *Handia* as an ancestor.

From that day onwards the grand father (paternal) is not given anything at the time of grand daughter's marriage. Only as bride price, along with bullock, a female calf is given and a *Khandanugulli* (a type of saree) is given to the mother.

Banana Tree - a Target

The Santals have an archery competition on the day following *Makar Sankranti*. In their language it is termed as

bheja tun. In this competition they keep one banana tree as the target of their arrow. This has been a tradition of the Santals.

Once upon a time a king was ruling over a kingdom. He had a queen. They did not have any children. The queen was in love with a black cobra before she got married to the king. After marriage she also used to visit that black cobra. Gradually the king came to know about it. One day the king went to the jungle for hunting but he stayed somewhere near the black cobra. He would hear the romantic conversation of the queen and her beloved. The king shot an arrow piercing the black cobra killing him at the spot. The queen's heart was overwhelmed with sorrow. Immediately there was a supreme command given to the queen 'bury my head infront of your entrance'. The queen after hearing this brought the cobra's head and buried it in front of the entrance. After a few days a tree sprouted at that spot. The queen was the only person who could recognise what that plant was. After the death of the black cobra there was always dispute and conflict between the king and the queen. The queen always tried to defeat the king in arguments by asking questions. Once the queen asked the king to tell the name of the plant present at the entrance. The king tried much, but in vain. The question was asked with a condition that anybody who failed to answer the same should be killed by piercing an arrow into his body. So at last the arrangement was made for piercing the arrow into the king by the people of that kingdom. The king called all his kith and kin for the last meeting before his death. The king's youngest sister's house was quite far off for which during the journey she had to take rest at several places. On one such occasion when she was taking rest with her children under a tree she heard a vulture on the tree speaking to her children on that tree. The vulture was saying 'children tomorrow you all will fly away from your nest in search of food' - The children asked their mother 'why tomorrow'. The mother immediately answered that 'tomorrow when the king would be killed I would get you human flesh. We have a tradition that after giving human flesh to the babies of the vulture, they have to move away from their nest, in search of their own food and that tradition is prevalent today also' - The baby vultures asked mother 'why is the king to be killed' ? The mother said 'there is a plant infront of the king's entrance. The queen had asked the name of the plant to the king and the king could not answer that question for which he is going to be killed. 'The baby vultures again asked 'what is the name of that plant ?' She replied 'that plant is a black cobra which was killed by the king'. This conversation was heard by the youngest sister of the king and she rushed to the king's palace. There at king's palace other tribes like Munda, Ho, along with Santals had gathered for piercing the arrow into the king's body. The king's sister after reaching secretly told the name of that plant to the king. As a result finally the king succeeded in giving the name of the plant to the queen. Now it was the turn of the queen to be killed by the bow and arrow. Everyone was waiting anxiously. The queen was placed at the king's place and the time came for releasing the arrow. But the queen's body suddenly disappeared and the plant existing near the entrance appeared at that place and the arrow got stuck into the plant. That plant was known by every one and it was named as *Kaira*. Today also in the Santal language that tree is called *Kaira*. According to the Santal language *Kaira* means banana and that was a banana tree. This incident had happened on the next day of Makar Sankranti. Therefore in the Santal community such archery competition of piercing a banana tree is still practised on that day.

Myth of Origin

Long ago the earth was completely covered with water which was an abode for the deities. Once they threw cotton into the water and it sank in the water. Then they threw pebbles into water which remained afloat. On one of those stones a plant grew which was named *Karam Siram*. The deities used to climb up and down on this *Karam Siram* plant with the help of a rope. Two birds named *Hons* and *Hanseli* built their nest on this plant and laid two eggs. Out of those eggs two *Manmis* took birth. After this the deities discussed among themselves and decided that though they were living in water but for both these '*Manmis*' (human beings) they had to get earth. Among the deities the Sun and moon were paramount. They called a meeting inviting all the gods and it was decided to take the opinion of kings of the nether regions.

First the tortoise king's opinion was taken. When they approached the tortoise he was smoking *hukka* on his throne. He was told that on that huge sheet of water cotton was thrown which sank whereas stones remained afloat. On one of such stones a plant grew on which two birds prepared their nest, out of whose eggs two Manmis took birth. For them they should prepare earth. Hearing this the tortoise king stated, 'no', I can not dig earth and carry them up. After this the sun God said, 'No' you will be fixed by four chains from four corners and food will be supplied near your mouth. We would only deposit soil on your back. Hearing this the king of tortoise consented. Further the Sun God asked regarding the other deities of nether land, so that they could be invited also. According to the information of the king of tortoise the deities approached the king of prawns and repeated the same story. Being persuaded by the deities the king of prawns lifted soil from the nether land and dropped on the back of the tortoise after which the king of crabs was invited to dig soil. Lastly the king of earthworms was called who helped the king of prawns to drop soil on the back of tortoise. In the process earth was created for which earth's crust was made plain. In some places there were insects which turned into forests, the higher regions became mountains and the gaps in between became rivers and streams. Finally the king of earthworms queried. 'This earth has been created for *Manmi*, what will you give me ? Both the sun and moon replied that earthworm would be guests in rainy season when their daughter would be married. This is the reason for which earthworms are mostly seen in rainy season.

Now earth was created. But the problem arose regarding the food for '*Manmi*' - They used to eat fruits and roots for their existence. One day Sun God gave them a root of one tree to eat which helped them to grow, on another day when the gods were moving in the forest they heard two birds gossiping and on enquiry they replied that they had gone to collect the root of a tree which when mixed with powdered rice and boiled the rice becomes intoxicating. Immediately one of the gods informed the matter to the *Manmis*. The *Manmis* prepared the aforesaid intoxicant and drank the same. Being intoxicated both the Manmis cohabited. As a result, twelve sons and twelve daughters were born. Both these *Manmis* were named as *Pilchubudhi* and *Pilchubudha*. One day *Pilchubudha* took the sons to forest and *Pilchubudhi* took the daughters to forest. Both the old people were lost in the forest and spent a lot of time there. In the meantime these twelve sons and twelve daughters cohabited which resulted expansion of their family. As a result each family became one clan totaling twelve clans as follows :-

1. Hansdah, 2. Murmu, 3. Khisku, 4. Baski, 5. Besra, 6. Tudu, 7. Hembrum, 8. Soren, 9. Marandi, 10. Core, 11. Pauria, 12. Chapea.

All these clans held meetings at several places to formulate rules and regulations. First, they went near the *Mahula* tree where nothing could be finalised for which *Mahula* tree is named as '*Khade-Matkam*'. Secondly, they went near the Banyan tree where also nothing was finalised for which is is called *'Peter bale'*. Thirdly, they went near the Kendu tree where also nothing could be finalised, for which it is called '*Lapez Tiril*'. Finally near the Sal tree all the rules and regulations could be formulated and it was named as Seri Sarjam which is worshipped by them till today. Gradually due to

expansion of family, they were divided into separate castes, as per the division of the articles existing in the family. One who took meat as a share, became Munda, Santal, Ho, etc. One who took coconut as a share, became Brahmin, one who took milk as a share became milkmen. In this manner as per the articles several castes originated.

SONGS

For Santals the leisure time is spent by dancing and singing. It is through this that they recreate themselves. When they have a satisfactory harvest, their feeling of joy and exhilaration find expression in songs and dances. Social and family gatherings and celebrations also give rise to songs and music. The songs reflect the lives of the tribals in all their variety and fullness. The anonymous folk songs are rich miniatures representing joys and sorrows of the village folk. They convey to us the aesthetic sense of the people. The unique feature about them is that they belong to the community. The authorship of the songs is not known to us. They are preserved by oral tradition.

In the journey of life from birth to death dance and music are closely associated. They get excited with the birth of a new baby. The birth of a girl child is more appreciated by the Santal society, because she fetches bride price. At the birth ceremony, the parents of the new born invite or welcome the guests to sing and dance by offering them rice beer. The dance which they do on this occasion is *lagene* i.e. dance for happiness. *Lagene* songs and dance are especially for happy moments or pleasure time. On the days of weekly markets they sing and dance for entertainment. Generally the Santal music has been classified in the following ways.

Classification of Santali Songs

Social Songs

Social songs are classified into name giving ceremony songs and marriage songs.

a) **Name Giving Ceremony Songs**
It is a cheerful time for all the family members. Generally when a baby is born a name giving ceremony is held which comes after 21 days of the birth of the child. The male child inherits either his paternal or maternal grand father's name while the female child inherits the name of the paternal or maternal grandmother's name. The marriage songs which are called *Dong* are sung near the new born baby on the day of the name giving ceremony.

b) **Marriage Songs**
Of all the types of marriages among the Santals Sange Bariyat marriage is the most important one. Along with this *Tunki, Dipil, Guldavnapam, Duar Itutee Sindur* marriages are also prevalent. In the *Sange Bariyat* marriage large number of people come from the bride groom's side. *Sange* according to the Santali language means more. *Bariyat* means people accompanying the bride groom. On the occasion of this marriage the boy instead of going to the girl's house will stay at his house. The kith and kin of the bride groom i.e. *Bariyat* will go to the girl's house to get her. While doing so they take along a bamboo stick and an umbrella as they consider these to be auspicious. *Tambour* is played for the purpose of singing and dancing. All the expenses in travel from the bride groom's house to the bride's house is borne by the bride groom's party or family. Before reaching the girl's house the male members of the bride's family asks

several riddles in the form of songs to the bride groom's party. This questioning through riddles and merry making staged on the day of marriage is called '*kudum*' in Santal language. *Kudum* is a kind of question answering competition which is done in the form of songs. If the groom's party is unable to answer those questions, then they are not allowed to enter the house for a short while. It is a time for fun and enjoyment and through this custom the bride's side has the opportunity to pull the legs of the groom's side. So in each stage as the bride groom's party moves forward they are asked several questions in the form of songs.

There are different types of marriage songs sung by these Santals from the stage of proposing till to the completion of the marriage. The marriage songs are classified as mentioned below.

(*i*) ***Balakala Serenj***

Before a marriage is fixed first the boy goes to see the girl and if he appreciates, then the family members from the girl's side will go to see the boy. The girl's parents take along a certain quantity of paddy and worship a

container full of water and also cover it with a bamboo basket before leaving for the boy's house. These are done to invite good omen. If they approve the boy then they sing the *Balakala Serenj*.

(*ii*) ***Bapla kudum Serenj***

At the time of *Sange Bariyat* the bride groom does not go to the bride's house to bring her, but the kith and kin from the groom's side go. They are asked several riddles in the form of song by the bride's family. They are welcome with respect from the entrance of the village. The riddles sung in the form of songs are called Kudum songs.

(*iii*) ***Binti Serenj***

The friends and relatives from the groom's side will reach the bride's house by answering several riddles asked to them. After reaching the bride's house they explain various myths and stories in the form of songs which are the Binti songs. There are songs on the origin of the earth, river, birds and animals etc.

(*iv*) ***Dang Serenj***

After Binti, the members from both bride and bride groom's side sing and dance together. This occasion is called *Dang*. Once the groom's party sing a song the bride's side again repeat the same.

Ritual Songs

These songs are classified into different types.

(i) ***Dahar Serenj***

The Santals celebrate different festivals in a year. The first festival when a year starts is *Mag Bonga* which is celebrated in the month of February. From this festival the Santal girls sing a type of song everyday till the festival of Baha Bonga, that is, the flower festival comes which usually falls after two or three weeks after *Mag Bonga*. These songs which

are sung just before the flower festival are known as *Dahar Serenj*, which reflect the different aspects of nature like river, forests, birds, animals, trees, fruits and flowers, etc. The songs have totally different lyrics which are easy to identify. Usually unmarried males and females sing these songs. But there is no strict rule. The married persons also sing them.

(ii) ***Baha Serenj***

These are sung on the day of flower festival. The priest sings several songs while worshipping and performing rituals. They invite deities by singing songs. Jaher Era is worshipped by making different kinds of offerings. Lastly they sing parting songs and give her farewell.

(iii) ***Rinja Serenj***

These are the songs sung on the *Gamha* festival when the cattle are worshipped.

(iv) ***Dasain Serenj***

These are the songs sung on the occasion of Durga Puja. They dance singing these songs. The puja starts from the seventh day and continues till the tenth day. They go out on a visit to the deities on the second day and return to their village on the seventh day. During all these days they sing and dance.

Besides the social and ritual songs there are agricultural songs, songs for happiness and other songs. Here in the following pages different songs sung by the Santals have been mentioned.

Example - 1

(i) ***Balakala Serenj***
Tahanreta Nana Tarena
Tahanreta Nana Tarena *i* (*A*)
Balakama Kalako Sakakama Sakako (*ii*)
Bandhubai Chekatepe Tayam Akan (*iii*)
Buruburu Parmare Gelbar Buru Parmare (*B*) (*i*)
Hati Bandhu Bhi A Janam Akanda (*ii*)
Handareka Dubau Akad Da (*iii*)
Balting Reka Duhiakad Da Bandhu Bhil, (*C*) (*i*)
Unigele Jnejnel Kana Bandu Bhai, (*ii*)
A Natele Tayam Akan (*iii*)

Meaning

The first line (A) (i) is the tune and the second line Balakama... Sakako (A) (ii).

Addressed to the parents of the bride and bride groom. Oh brothers and sisters why are you late ? Crossing the forests, ten to twelve forests. Elephant has given birth to kith and kin, Curd was made in a bucket, brother and sister that was only we had seen. That was only we had drunk. Because of that we were late.

(ii) ***Dong Serenj***

Kalikatare Michin Barpadare Bairi
Kuli Anare Bandhuka Sade Gud Gud
Ama Mam Manag Akan
Ani Mani Tayam Akan
Tangi Ini Me Alam Bagiani

Meaning

Machine is at Calcutta,
Enemies are at Baripada
Guns are being fired at Kuliana,
You are leading and I am behind you
Wait for me and do not go
leaving me behind

Example - 2

Akakhanach Aayal Hejen Aka Khanach Banand Hejen
Hay Purte Banand Bhundte Chene Tukey Papud Unjur
Kei Chene Hukin Bhidau R Kin Aphir Balay
Tuka Hukin Hal Balay Hapan Jalate (2)

Meaning

From which side wind blows
From which side storm came
With the force of the wind and
storm the bird's nest was blown away.
The birds are moving here and there in sorrow
Mother bird is busy in building a nest for a better
condition of her babies.

(iii) *Janam Baba Janam Aya Injbin*
Janam Lidinj
Jiwire Paleo Lagao Ena Sua
Sengel Bati
Marang Baru Jaher Aya, Abinthen Ge Raga Injad
Hisa Suya Sengel
Batidey Dantim Harsul Kabin
Sarag Rinij Sirjan Enjid Tapaj
Mane Day
Tapa Keya, Balang Jnapam Rehen
E Dulal
Injlan Balang Hilinj
Alo Sego Raga Hulal, Alo Sego
Hamra
Hidir Hidir Kalam Chetan Mejda
Alo Semgo Jar Ah.

Meaning

O my mother, father, you had given birth to me
I am becoming envious.
O Maran Buru Jaher Era I beg you, save me
If the heaven's Creator will reco ncile with us, then we would be able to talk to each other even if we do not marry.

Bapla Kudum Serenj

(1) *Nande Menah X Majhi*
Nande Menah Y Majhi
X Majhi Marang Kala
Bapla Mente Hejleya
Sai Sai Ma Taka Emlet
Bishsai Ma SanaEmlet
Rehat Hna Gajgeya
Dugi Hna Gajgeya
Tabe Da Baba Nali Kana
Unige Harde Aset Ket
Etam Tehna Harda Menha
Kanje Tehna Harda Menha
Oka Hartepe Param Chalha
Sange Bariyat

Meaning

Here is X Majhi (Sacred head)
There is Y Majhi
X Majhi is wealthy
He has come only for marriage
Hundreds of rupees he gave
Twenty hundred pieces of gold he gave
The rope is broken
The cow is dead
Still it goes
This is what has obstructed the road
Road is on the left
Road is on the right
In which road will the bride groom's relatives go ?

Some additional Santal songs and the particular aspects of Santal living in which the songs are used are listed below.

1. Cultivation songs (Horo Rothwe)
2. Forest songs (Bir Seren) giving early years of a person. It may be mentioned that forest songs are needed on various occasions where love has been the dominant theme and occasions like Bitlaha, marriage, Sohrae represent forest songs.
3. Induction of the tribe (Caco chatier)
4. Social dances accompany songs such as 1. Lagre songs through which a boy or girl after his/her induction joins the dances of the adults on various occasions; 2. Dahar songs concerning village romance; 3. Godwari songs used in Vulture dance moving in a circle and 4. Dasae songs used in dances representing pantomime and trance postures.
5. Marriage songs (Don seren) depicting love and affection.
6. Songs relating to conflicting situations which arise during marriage proposals.
7. Typical songs which are used on different stages of marriage, family life, breakdown of negotiation, divorce etc.
8. Karama songs
9. Dawn songs (Bhimsar)
10. Songs related to wanted child
11. Bonga story songs and Bonga lover songs
12. Women at work songs
13. Witches songs
14. Animal hunt songs
15. Death songs
16. Mourning songs

Cultivation songs

(Santal song P. 22-23 'The Hill of Flutes')

1. *Wealth, wealth*
Where is your mother ?
Where is your father ?
My mother and father
Are wind and rain
My milk is water trickling

2. *Wealth, wealth*
O mother wealth
Where was your birth ?
I was born
In the splash of rain.

3. *The paddy is weeping*
The paddy is asking
When will be my wedding ?
When the water of the sky
Drenches the earth
Then will be your wedding.

4. *In our fields*
In our lands
Is a house of wealth.

Lagre type

1. *There are ten drummers*
There are twenty girls
The dancing ground is big and wide
Do not rouse me, drummer
Or I will make you drink
A river-full of water.

2. *The fly-catcher, elder brother*
Is crying out of water.
All things are bad, girl

3. *At night I slept on a verandah*
And in a dream I found you
How lovely you were
Swaying in the dew.

4. *O you peacock in the peacock forest*
I will make you fly
On your feathers I will put
Golden sindur

5. *To the high lands*
Went the cattle
To the muddy swamp
The buffaloes
Middle brother,
The mud is heaving
In the gully with the plantains
Is a spring with a bonga

6. *Monkey, from branch to branch you sprang*
You strolled from path to path
Take care, monkey
Or the citron fruit will fall

7. *In the middle of the street*
Is a dancing ground
Go quickly, girl
For though your are frightened
I shall look inside your heart.

8. *With a gold umbrella*
You have gone away, my son
But do not cross
The five mountains
Let me go, mother
Go I will

For a girl is standing
Lovely as a flame

Dahar type

1. *In a bush of thorns*
Two pigeons
Are busy with a nest
Boy
Do not shoot an arrow
For the two
Are calling to each other

2. *On the mountain the flames spread*
On the hill the fire
Goes mounting in a line
Look at that old man
Running and stumbling
Look at that boy
And the lily
Straining into bud

3. *Climb on the thatch, girls*
See him on his way
For he goes, he goes
To the foot of the mountain.

4. *Mother*
On the small hill
I gathered cotton
And my ring
Slipped from my finger

5. *Behind an ant-hill is a porcupine*
We will stone him from above
We will pelt him till he falls.

6. *Beyond the mountain*
The ring dove is cooing
Under the mountain
The boys are with the cattle
With a flute they struck the dove
O my friend, go slowly
Very slowly.

7. *Durgi*
Your brother-in-law
Has climbed a fig tree
Durgi
Your brother-in-law
Is being chased by bees.

Golwari type

1. *The vultures circle in the sky*
O vulture, give me wings like yours
And I will fly like you

2. *The peacocks feed on scorpions and snakes*
O peacock, give me wings like yours
And I will dance like you

3. *O quail, quail*
Give me a song like yours
And I will sing like you

Dasae type

1. *Girl, how lovely you look*
With your dress clinging
How lovely you look
With your cloth
Rucked in folds

2. *On the path the pipal fruit is ripe*
And the pied mainas cry cero bero
The green twist their heads.

3. *Parrot, do not cry*
At the pain in your body
Do not mourn
In the bar tree by the road
Your father and mother
Are high up on the mountain
Dove, your father and brothers
Are out in the forest.

4. *In the forest the birds twitter*
In the village the girls sing

5. *Two girls like sticks*
With winding curves
O two girls
Stamp on the pounder
Clean the rice in a fan
O two girls
Listen to the bangles
Listen where the pounder cells
O two girls
Finish your rice
Finish making that curry

6. *O you two girls*
In a big house
With rounded thatch
Comb your tresses
Tie them in a knot
The Dasae boys are upon you
You must take their greetings

7. *O you two girls*
Bathing in the river
You are scrubbing your hair with earth
The string of a necklace is drifting down
As you catch the string, the sun is setting

8. *In the river, the fish glitter*
In the stream, the fish shine
In the big village, the girls are flashing

9. *Going, I went and saw*
Looking and I looked
As the water brimming in the well
The water gushing from the spring.

10. *In the river, the alligator*
Slashes with its tail
In the village the boys
Swagger up and down.

11. *Mother, give me my loin-cloth*
Give me my fiddle
I am going, mother
To wander in the country
I am going, parrot
To rove about the land

12. *On the road the traders*
Are raising the dust
In the village street
The Dasae boys are romping

13. *At the village end is a bar tree*
With a sound of bells
The two teachers met
The bells are jangling
The dust mixes
From the kicking feet

14. *Guru, for many days*
    You ruled your pupils
    Now I will blind you like a dove
    I will trap you like a quail

15. *Guru, your right foot*
    On a line of gossamer
    Guru, your left foot
    On a fiddle's bow.

16. *In a gold cloth*
    Is the Guru's wife
    She is sitting in a chair
    She is looking in a glass
    And like a lotus leaf
    She moves her head

Love songs

(Santal song P. 130-132 'The Hill of Flutes')

1. *Black dog, stop barking*
   It is only my friend
   Like a hungry tiger or a leopard
   He is slinking around

2. *Yesterday you said*
   We will go out
   When the morning star has come
   Today the sun is up
   And still you do not come
   In the garden
   I have leant against a mango
   And shut my eyes

3. *The time has come*
   The time to have each other

My friend is going on the plantation grove
For my friend is tired of waiting

4. *At noon we said*
But you come at midnight
You are knocking the legs of the bed
O my love, move very slowly
The father and brothers
Have their axes and arrows ready
They will wake and seize us

5. *O my love*
With an axe like a fan
And arrows like thatch
Is my brother coming
O my love
Let my life go
And my head fall
But never will I leave your love

6. *You in the upper village*
I in the lower
O my love
My heart is tied to you
Your father and brothers
Are standing with axes and arrows
But, my love
You do not make my heart sad
With thick creepers
The tree is hidden
You have glued me to you
Like a bird trapped in lime.

Wedding songs

1. *In our courtyard*
Is a sweet tarmarind

Its branches are large
Its flowers are white and red
Its fruits hang in clusters

2. *Below our field*
Are many coloured flowers
Come to our village, boy
And choose what flower you will

3. *Still you are little, girl*
But the friends are choosing you
Where are your father and mother ?
O 'haere haere hae'
My mother and father are not here
They have gone to the mountain
To knock the mahua down.

4. *My parents are like the moon*
My brothers and sisters are like stars
O my flower
Why was I not made
A flaming fire ?

5. *In that big house, girl*
You had everything you wanted
Put out of your mind
Your teeth's powder
And the black for your eyes
Do not think
Of your bath in the morning.

6. *While you are unmarried girl*
You laugh and smile
While you are unmarried
You have the love of a friend
When the silver ring

Will go on your finger
It will change your life.

7. *Slim as the mountain grass I grew*
But as I grew
I left behind my joy

Divorce songs

(Santal song P. 214-215 'The Hill of Flutes')

1. *Friend, we have left going*
To the rice field in the jungle
They have given you a wife
They have found for me a husband
O my friend, when we meet now
we must never flutter our eyebrows
Or show the teeth in our mouths

2. *O my love, do not weep*
Do not mourn
I will come and go
And share your love

3. *Sister, that young boy*
He did not leave me
Even in his wedding litter
He was making eyes at me

4. *In a litter, in a palki, father*
You brought me a wife
But though you brought her
I will not leave
My village girl.
O daughter-in-law
You whom we have brought
Why are you weeping ?

5. *I went by paths*
I met her in the way
She said
Give me a red flower

6. *Seeing the milk flower, mother*
I picked and put it in my hair
I broke the stem
The tree withered
That boy
Has taken away my heart

Bonga lover

(Santal song P. 279 'The Hill of Flutes')

1. *At noon I went for water*
I met a bonga or a boy
If you are bonga, drag yourself away
If you are lover, stay with me and [illegible]

Kiya baha campa baha
Nagudarae me-ho mairi.
Husband— *Nagu mairin naguam*
Cal mairin catam
Cekatem bahaya
Cekatem baha mosoda
Wife— *Nin reak' bud mairi*
Nin reak' nakil
Cauric' ren gutuya
Bohok' ren baha mosoda

Meaning

This song is a conversation between a husband and a wife, and sung during the Sohrae festival. The wife asks the husband to bring Keya and Campa flowers for her while going to the big hill for hunting. The husband assures her to bring those flowers but asks her whether she knows the art of using them. The wife responds by saying that she is clever and wise, and she will decorate her hair with these flowers.

2. *Deho durup'pe*
Deho tengonpe,
Jomak' nunyak' boeh, banuk' taleya
Met' nepal boeha ahajiba
Akal kedae gaten sawanek' edae
Ita ranu gaten bale nawana
Sanam hoponin ko dingra cabayen
Kiminin ho kiminin
Kursa baha kiminin
Kiminin ranu gedo ban namlet
Pai pailan nataekeda
Bandi horon nalaeket'
Kiminin mon gedo pan namlet

Meaning

This song is usually sung on the concluding day of the Sohrae. It welcomes a visitor and describes about agricultural distress. It also narrates the situation further where the visitor is told as to how a beautiful girl could not be brought home as bride because of paucity of money during this distress period.

Marriage songs

(Santal song P. 208-209 'The Santals')

1. *Cetan disomren sange baryat,*
   Bare hutarebon deraket'ko;
   Jomak' nuniak' do timinrecon
   Bare hongor hatar metakope

Meaning

This song is a marriage song which has a humorous description about a bridegroom's party. The bridegroom's party has reached the village and they are taking rest under a banyan tree. A suggestion is given that they should eat banyan fruit while taking rest because no body knows when the dinner will be served to them.

2. *Beker beker yamgim janamlidin,*
   Konor konor yamgim haralidin,
   Batire basan dak' malire sunum
   Koto jotonte yamgim haralidin.
   Bam dayalenayo bammayalen
   Lela ninda minhun merom
   Lela yamgim chutikidin.

Meaning

The emotion and feelings of a bride during her departure from her people is decribed in this song. She is also reminded of the care and affection given by her mother during her childhood.

Love of Flowers and Birds

(Santal song P. 214 'The Santals')

1. *Maran buru cotre*
Berdor bahado jenget jenget
Malinan metaya baha lan koyeya
Berdor bahado jenget jenget.

Meaning

The desire of a group of people for Berdar flower has been described in this poem. They want to ask the gardener to give them these deep-red flowers which are found on the top of a hill.

SANTAL LEGEND

1 *Setahre Bered Tara Gada Dah Junj Senlena*
Gate Kulik Lananj Kana Gata Da Bany Gijah Aa.. (2)
Sen Kateni Enjel Kede Talama Racharek Adink Akad
Parkam Perejka Sajao Aka Degjiwi Rinij Gate (2)
Atu Rege Jira Majhid Atu Ma Mane Halak
Inj Thenge Galar Gameha Injthenge Harmala
Akare Gunj -
Kulihma Kulihte Kulhima Talate
Kulihma Atunkaher
Andege Gunj Emama Dulal Jiwi Rinij Gate (2)

Meaning

In the early morning I had gone to bring water from the river-my girl friends told me that my lover is no more in this world. I went and saw he was lying on a bed and had been decorated with flowers and with turmeric paste and oil anointed on him.

There are five other people in this village and what should I give you. I have only this towel and necklace. What should I give to my life partner.

In front of the village, I will give every thing to my life partner.

2. *Kulih Kulihte Linjin Kana*
Jharana Dayad : Jharana Dayad
Kala Baded Geya : (2)
Al Kalape Enjua Jharana Bad
Jharana and Kala Bade Geya

Meaning

The boys are informed through commands about the waterfall which is flowing on the way, the water of which is polluted and they should not drink it.

The Santal youths go to other villages at night to dance and thus they talk to their lovers there. This is considered polluted.

Daher Serenj

Mangal Bandi Senlena Dem
Kamid Adihar Ket Ah
Gate Bhai Dhiri Dipil (2)
Gada Tahenkan Gadak Esetked
Dare Tahenkan Darek Bhindal Ked
Daha Da Linjien Kenal Kenal Te (2)
Daha Da Linjien Chehel Bahel (2)
Daha Da Linjien Janam Disamte (2)

Meaning

The girl had gone to do brick loading work at Mangalbandi near Bihar. She saw brick loading work was going on there and seeing that she thought it to be a very difficult work.

River was there and a bridge was constructed over it. Trees were cut down. Water was carried through land. Water started flowing in a rhythmic way and it flows to the land of the earth.

2. *Ingpil Ichchahbabr Lahkan*
Janumpil Janumbabu Lakhan
Sermare Raja Channu Lah Kan
Delababu Raja Darbar
Atare Ma Janum, Sere Mere Ma Damparengeini
Sun Kenjme Madan Malki Bengal Janum Da.

Meaning

Ingpil and Janumpil are the two areas situated at Chaigal and Champagal near Bihar. Fire broke out in those two hills, that is, riots started. The Santals informed this to the king of heaven and requested him to go to the place and while going to the place the thorns on the ground and the Bheji brinjal from heaven pricked into their feet. The Santals took out the thorn with the help of Bheji Brinjal thorn.

3. *Janam Aaya Daya Dulal San A Tharire Dakay Emany*
Sana Ginare Utuya Emanj
Kaki Aya Hisa Saya Kay Batire Daka Emanj
Rahal Sakam Re Utay Emanj

Meaning

The real mother who has given birth gives rice in the golden plate, curry in the golden bowl. While stepmother being envious gives rice on a plate similar to the plate of a beggar and gives curry on dry leaves.

Dance and music are the part and parcel of Santal life. They sing and dance and enjoy each and every moment during festivities. The different types of dances are as follows :

Baha Dance

As its name signifies this is danced during the Baha flower festival on the second day. Men and women of the

SANTAL DANCE

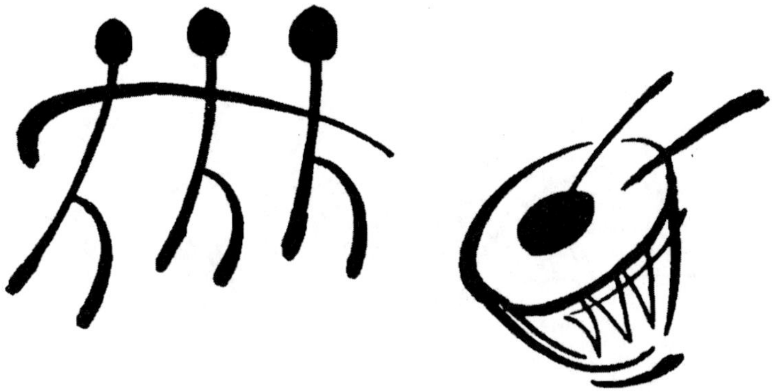

tribe go to the sacred grove (*Jaherthan*) accompanied by the village priest, to invoke the deities there. This is also a devotional dance in which only women take part. They do not inter-lock their hands, form no circles, but proceed in matching order with musicians in a separate group. As they go on, men sing and women reply in chorus, it is picturesque to see the dancers waving their right hands upwards, up to the shoulders, which are swung down soon to be folded beautifully. When the right hand is raised the right foot takes a step. Next advance the left foot and the folded hands are raised up with devotional beam in their eyes. So they go on till they reach the Holy Grove and thus dance round it thrice. '*Baha*' is also danced when the village priest returns home with the flowers on the final day of the flower festival.

Dang Dance

This dance is generally performed during marriage. Men and women choose their groups and form a lively

circle. The women interlock their hands gracefully, whereas, men with *nagera* and *madal* stand in the centre forming an inner circle. As the music continues, the dancers advance two steps to the right in a general motion. Next they dance for twenty minutes or so, while women sing in unison. When the dance is finished, it is now men's turn to sing, while women reply in a musical chorus. This goes on for sometime, when again the drums resound, the country side echoes and re-echoes with a merry din and the dance starts afresh. So they dance on and on in a two-day long non-stop manner.

This dance may also take place as a mark of joy when volunteers help a Santal farmer who has to get helping hands in his agricultural operations.

Dahar Dance

This dance takes place sometime between the first day after the new moon of *Magh* (January-February) and the full moon of *Falgun* (February-March) beginning in the evenings and ending at mid nights, the musicians standing in the centre. One sees the circle taking two steps forward and then changing the direction to the left and step next to the right again with a single step. The circle thus moves on and on in the dreamland of a moonlit night. Men sing and women reply jointly.

Lagene

This is the most common Santal dance and may be held at any time, but a moonlit night is the favourite occasion for it. When the moon glimmers, men beat the drums and *madals* to attract the youths and maids of the tribe by the music. Soon sufficient number of partners assemble at the spot. They then make a complete circle with a radius of seven to ten feet. The steps of the *lagene* dance are regular and although they wave the feet forward making an angle and swing to the right while the circle appears to move in an anti-clockwise direction.

RIDDLES

Just for a change from grazing cattle, playing games, or assisting in the house, Santal children amuse themselves with riddles. These forms of verbal play do not have any special functions but spring from euphemisms and kennings which liberally besprinkle tribal talk.

Certain symbols for example are constantly being used for avoiding the unpleasant sad and painful expressions. A Santal, who sees that an old man's teeth are decaying, does not refer directly to the teeth but says the white pebbles are falling or the grinding stones are wanting. When someone dies the villagers do not mention death but say he has gone down to the ground, he has gone to herd the alligators, he got tired, fled away and has gone across. A Santal, who goes out in the dark hours of the morning, does not say that he intends to urinate he simply says that he is going to the courtyard to open the outlet of a tank.

Similar verbal expressions refer to other aspects of life like marriage, child birth etc. But besides these expressions which gently or jokingly dispose of difficulties, the Santals also employ a number of kennings. These are used when too direct a reference to the subject is believed to harbour danger.

These types of riddle speech are such a common thing that the Santals practise that formal riddles or *kudums* are sometimes hardly distinguishable. Their main difference is one of form whereas a riddle phrase or a kenning comes naturally into conversation, a formal riddle is always supposed to be a question and to need a quick and rapid answer. Boys and girls use them, in fact, as tests of wit, as ways of demonstrating each others cleverness. Yet although amusement is the primary object, riddles are not without importance for later life. They bring remote concepts into mutual irritation. They reveal fantastic similarities and emphasize unusual parallels. They accustom the children in fact, to thinking in images and when in due course they learn the village songs, they are immediately at home with their complicated symbolism. The *kudum* is the Santal child's unconscious introduction to poetry.

In the following riddles, details of landscape, day to day sights and sounds, aspects of village life and general Santal behaviour are widely depicted.

1. *Kudum Re Kulit Kulit*
Duletka Del Jangpe
Ingde Kulchung Kate Gujuanj

Meaning

Boy : go away (*Kundali* Sag)

2. *Kudum Re Kulit Kulit*
Gel Hal Sendrak Chatawa
Mit Phalk Agua, Anadachet (Katkam)

Meaning

Ten people go for hunting and will bring one half (Crab).

3. *Erre Ita Banua, Jamre Jang Banua*

   Meaning
   No seed to sow, no bone to eat (Mushroom)

4. *Matang Buning Chene, Mid Gina Dahre Unum Gujua*

   Meaning
   One small bird drowns in little water (Sulung or salt).

5. *Akatena Bah Anij Nate Mena Bang Bahaenij - (Har Katkam)*

   Meaning
   Which party with head, which party without head (Tortoise, Crab)

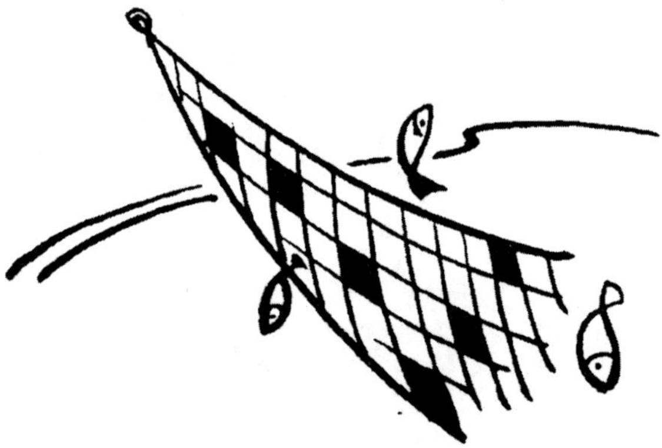

6. *Gada Gadate Lanb Lanb (Jalam)*

   Meaning
   Scattered over the river here and there (Net)

7. *Sirili Birili Sakamre Kadam Phoolda (Chala)*

Meaning
Big fruits on small leaves (Yellow gram)

8. *Dela Budhi Pund Dungri Param Gatkainjnlin Ante Da Initege Chalwa (Dakajam)*

Meaning
O ! old mother help me cross the mountain
I will go alone across the mountain (Rice eating)

9. *Ankalu Bankuln Dal Baisu Siren Cart (Ahthara)*

Meaning
A curved stick (Walkable road)

10. *Myd Hala Daie Enech Kana Bahya*
Tala Rachare Mane Halteka Nel Kana
Pun Haladaka Ukua Kana (Daktagasao)

Meaning

One man is dancing in the middle of the courtyard, five persons are watching and four persons have hidden themselves (Tobacco).

11. *Bahukulia Menete Sakam Re*
Peya Gar Da Bahiya Ched Ched Ka Kana
Anage Baba Har Da Esed Kawa

Meaning

The daughter-in-law wears a type of bangle with three lines on it. These three lines signify-firstly to get respect in society, secondly, to give respect to the deities, thirdly to get respect from their Santal culture.

PROVERBS

Westermarck has defined 'the proverbs of the people in W.G. Archer's book "The Hills of flutes" as these valuable documents concerning their character, temperament, opinions, feelings, manners and customs. They are not only reflections of life, they also play an active part in it. Most proverbs are expressions of feelings or opinions or are intended to influence people's wills and actions".

The majority of Santal proverbs are similes that either they point out a moral or enshrine a tribal experience.

1. *Dina Da Chalah Dinada Ruahla*
   Rupad Chalah Rapad Baya Rualla
   Kansa Pitala Leka Dul Aruganah Khandah
   Rupad Hanang Dul Arua.

   Meaning :

   Days will go and come. But grace once gone will never come; grace is just like the brass utensils.

2. *Aama Bugi Legit Teche Halch Makiana*
   Agan Rabang Khetir Teche Nindai Situng Ama

   Meaning

   Will others do your work for your good : Will the cold night of winter become day ? (An opportunist person).

3. *Hamal Rawal Tula Lekhan Rawal Chataha*
   Huding Halch Maranglen Khan Senahin Leluha

   Meaning

   A heavy and light thing if weighed then the lighter side goes high. If the poor one becomes rich then he tries to make false vanity.

4. *Seta Bapulang Da Sekil Sakam Rinij*
Hatah EE Har Mala, Bange Sabhaa

Meaning

Dogs place is at the waste food. The gold chain shines at the neck of an appropriate person with status.

These are so explicit that comment is unnecessary. Sometimes a few proverbs attempt to see both sides. 'You cannot cook a cake one side up'. While deciding a dispute a village must hear the other man. Similarly, you can not clap with one hand. The headman alone cannot decide a quarrel but the whole village must assist.

Finally there are a few proverbs that comment on sex and marriage. These are of great importance. A proverb such as "A feathered arrow drives straight" is almost unintelligible without reference to the songs. Its meaning is that marriage keeps a husband constant. But in order to express this point it has to take recourse in poetry. Not only is the arrow a stock poetic symbol for a potent lover but by referring to a wife as 'feathers' the proverb conjures up two other Santal images the peacock with its tail (the image in poetry for a young unmarried girl) and an image from ordinary life, the clothes of a girl haunched like feathers over her haunches.

SANTAL METAPHOR

The Santal oral literature consists many metaphors. Some common metaphors are given below.

1. *Tarup Mancha* : Loud voice
2. *Kayel Alang* : Cuckoo's voice
3. *Kahu Alang* : Harsh voice
4. *Hadar Hay* : Dry wind
5. *Bayar Kada* : A violent man
6. *Del Harkam* : Frickle
7. *Tadi Daa* : Spring water
8. *Hisid Hisid Hay* : Soothing breeze
9. *Hipil Hipil Jar* : Waving flag
10. *Raput Tukuj* : Women divorcee
11. *Mut Dumda* : Talkative
12. *Mahu Tuka* : Crow nest (the head of the women)
13. *Usal Buru Leka* : Nose like a big mountain
14. *Kulih Hala* : Idle person

CONCLUSION

Additional texts about the talents of Santals regarding folklore of the Santals..

It is necessary to mention a few words about the songs and dances of the Santals who bear many distinctive characters. They are so much attached to singing and dancing that W.G. Archer has given the title of his book on the portrait of the Santals as "The Hill of Flutes". In the preface he has introduced the Santals as "the most integrated and possibly the most resilient tribe in Eastern India. Their love of dancing and singing, their splendid physique, the airy freedom, with which both men and women go about and their belief in *bongas* or nature-spirits complex remind the observer of ancient India; and their love poetry-simple, sensuous and passionate-shared with that of Kalidasa, Amaru and Jayadeva speak of the early Indian attitude to sex".

There are innumerable types of songs which are sung on different occasions. Some of these types are reproduced from Archer's book, "The Hill of Flutes".

1. Cultivation song (*Horo Rothwe*),
2. Forest song (*Bir Seren*),
3. *Caco Chatiar* song,
4. *Lagre* songs,
5. *Dahar* songs,
6. *Golwari* songs,
7. *Dasae* songs,
8. Marriage songs (*Don Seren*),
9. *Bitlaha* songs,
10. *Sohrae* songs (*Danta*), (*Dhurumjak*),
11. Baha songs,
12. *Karam* songs,
13. Dawn songs (*Bhinsar*),
14. Bonga story songs,

15. Witches' songs,
16. Annual Hunt songs (*Bir Seren*),
17. Mourning songs,
18. *Mora Karam* songs.

Archer has characterized the Santals as "the ever-singing Santali". What he has said about the Santali songs and Santali poetry are reproduced below.

'The ever-singing Santals'

Besides T.H. Lewin, E.G. Man (an Assistant Commissioner in the Santal Parganas) sensed the important part played by poetry in Santal life :

"There is a dash of poetical feeling in the composition of the Sonthals (He wrote in 1867) which shows itself in their traditions. Their songs generally allude to birds and flowers and unlike the lyrics of their neighbours are remarkably free from obscenity. The tunes also which they play on their flutes are often attempts at imitation of the notes of birds or have a wild melancholy cadence, which heard in the depths of the jungle, sounds pleasing on the ear. The following is the song of a love-sick girl".

"The Osprey's voice is heard on the mountain
Then the people feel pity
Oh, mother, at midnight, the peacock's tail
Can be seen on the top of the hills and in the valley
My brother observes the white flower
Upon the dried-up tree
The parrot has her young ones
Oh, aunt, when will you dandle my children ?
When will you, my aunt ?
The cock crows in the morning

Oh, my mother, come and see it
From the steep sides of the mountain
I hear a pair of flutes
And below in the valley
The beating of a drum".

"This was not the only song that Man recorded. During a camp at Simra he attended a Santal wedding and as a consequence passed a sleepless night for as soon as the males had become too unsteady in gait or voice to dance and sing, the women took their places and until long after cock crow refrains were borne to my unwilling ears as I lay and tossed on my cot".

"The full meaning of these songs was not perhaps realised by Man and it is also obvious that a whole category of Santal poetry-the *Bir Seren* or Forest songs-escaped him. None the less, in referring to a dash of poetical feeling in the composition of the Santals', he had made a crucial point". (The Hill of Flutes ps. 343-344)

SANTALI POETRY

What Man has mentioned about Santali poetry are reproduced below.

"Printed collections of Santali songs in original Santali are listed in the bibliography - the chief collections being Hor Seren and Don Seren, published jointly by Gopal Gamaliel Soren and myself in 1943. Hor Seren comprises 1676 songs which are sung at festivals or dances, Don Seren 1824 songs which are sung at weddings. A further 129 cultivation songs are included in the second volume. The majority of these songs are ancestral but it is part of the vitality of Santal poetry that new songs are sometimes made up on the spur of the moment. There is no special class of poet, singer or bard, and the songs are accordingly communal in origin and inspiration. Songs connected with the induction ceremony of *Coco Chatiar* and with the ritual of *Karam* are given in Stephen H. Murmu's *Karam* or *Caco Chatiar* (published 1945). The special songs, known as *Bir Seren*, which are sung in the privacy of the forest, are as yet unpublished. A manuscript collection amounting to almost one thousand is with me and I hope in due course to deposit it in the India Office Library, London. Songs of this kind are characterised by a bold use of sexual terms and for this reason are banned in Santal villages. They fall into two categories-those which are tender, sensitive and charming, the prerogative of women, girls and lovers and those which are coarse and bawdy, the 'music-hall' entertainments which are put on at *bitlahas* and at annual hunts. *Bir Seren*, intended primarily for lovers, could well be termed 'Forest Love Songs', *Bir Seren* which are primarily jocular could be termed 'Forest Hunt songs'. Since the same title cover both sorts, it is no surprise that, as one Santal expressed it, 'to the old, Bir Seren are jokes but to the young, they are beauty'.

"All Santal songs, whether 'forest' or 'village', have certain characteristics. Rhyme is not employed and the form of the song, the length of its lines and indeed its whole structure is determined to a great extent by the tune or melody. Few songs have more than ten or twelve lines; any that are longer have usually a ritual purpose. In some cases the fourth line repeats the second but more normally every line is different and the song achieves its effect by a subtle combination of assonance, rhythm and imagery. In one important respect, the use of unexplained symbols, Santal poetry is very close to that of the Uraons, samples of which I translated in my books, The Blue Grove and the Dove and the Leopard. Just as in English slang, 'girls' are called 'birds', so in Santali 'girls' are often 'peacocks', children 'Little parrots', mother 'milk trees', boys 'flutes' and so on. It is to the vivid character of particular symbols that many Santal songs owe their poetic brilliance".

"For translation, I have adopted the following principles. When working on Uraon poetry, I had modelled myself on Arthur Waley and believing, like him, that 'images were the soul of poetry',. I had refrained both from using rhyme and from 'either adding images of my own or suppressing those of the original'. The same method had been independently arrived at by Verrier Elwin, first in his songs of the Forest, a collection that he published with Shamrao Hivale in 1935 and later in the Baiga. We were aware however that not every previous translator adhered to these principles and when in 1942 we began to edit the Indian journal of anthropology, Man in India, I was led to preface a short anthology of Indian folk-poetry with the following editorial".

"If translations are to be of value, it is obvious that they should conform to certain standards. The most evident is that the translation should itself be a poem. If it is not a poem, if it does not create the effect of poetry, it is merely a degradation of its original, an act of murder. The second requisite is that the translation should correspond with the original. If it does not correspond, it loses all claim to scientific value. It ceases to be the translation of a poem. It becomes a poem by a translator. Such a poem may have value as poetry but it has none at all as science. The problem of translating Indian folk poetry is in essentials how to produce a version which contains all the elements both of poetry and science".

"It will be evident that to this problem no solution will be perfect. A poem is a combination of certain images, certain rhythms and certain effects of music, and only if a translation could provide an exact parallel for each of these elements could it be perfect. In actual fact, a translation from a tribal language into English can parallel only one of these elements. Differences of verbal structure are so great that if parallel images are retained, the rhythms will be different. If the rhythms are maintained, the images will suffer, while no form of English can reproduce the musical effects of Hindi, Oraon, *Gondi* or *Mundari*. 'Certain things', said *Ezra Pound*, "are translatable from one language to another, a tale or an image will translate; music will practically never translate. "A translation becomes possible, therefore, only when there is no attempt at all at complete correspondence".

"We believe that the best solution so far reached is that of Arthus Waley. In translating from Chinese Arthus Waley was faced with problems that are identical with those of Indian languages. His solution has been a series of versions in which the literal meaning of the translation corresponds with the literal meaning of the original. In particular, the images are never added to and never subtracted from. The poem as a system of images remains in translation what it is in the original. Instead, however, of attempting a duplication of rhyme, rhythm or music, his versions use the rhythms and sound effects which come most naturally to English. The original form is abandoned and instead the effort is to create a new form which is valid for a contemporary sensibility. We believe that in terms of this solution translations of Indian folk poetry can preserve all the elements essential for anthropology while still retaining all the ingredients of poetry".

This editorial was published in March 1943, four months after I reached the *Santal Parganas*. I can not hope that all the present versions successfully achieve these standards. But they do, at least, attempt to reach them. I have not distorted the literal meaning of any of the originals and I have not added or left out any image or symbol".

"There remains the question of how best to present these versions. It would have been possible to group them according to the occasions on which they were used and to add notes explaining their imagery. But this, I think would have weakened their impact. Santal poetry is Santal life; Santal life is Santal poetry. I decided, therefore to employ two methods and to alternate between them. If a song illustrated with special vividness a particular aspect of Santal living, I have used it as evidence of thought, feeling or behaviour and removed it from its social context. In the accounts of marital and premarital love, for example, I have freely inserted wedding, *Sohrae* and Forest love songs. If on the other hand, certain songs or stories are essential parts of a ceremony such as the *Karam*, or of a festival such as the *Baha*, I have presented them in their original setting. The result may not be wholly satisfactory but the following chart will, I hope make clear my underlying method".(The Hill of Flutes ps. 344-346)

Among these tribal groups quite a large part of ethnic music is ritualistic. These are the invocation songs, the ritual incantations meant for certain formalistic worship accompanied by the sacrifice of animate objects and/or other 'offerings'. The same applies to the group of invocation songs of the Santals known by the generic name of *Bakhens*. Here we are giving the translation of some of the invocation songs collected from the book *"Bakhen"* written by Pandit Raghunath Murmu.

Bakhen

1. Salutation to you, Mother *Jaher Era*.
On the occasion of *Magh* festival we offer you,
The delicate chicks, the freshly husked rice and
it is required for you to accept and listen our prayers.
On the starting of New Year and with the entry of new products and incidents, you have to decide them and welcome them.
The Sal and Mahul plants are to be full of flowers and fruits all over and you have to create them.
We will pluck the wild leaves and sag from the forest and the wild grass for the thatching of the house.
You have to supply them in plenty.
The tigers and tigresses are to be brought under control.
Kalke Jamun (a type of bush), *Lat Jamun* (a type of wild bush), creepers must be spread all around - which are to be pressed down.
Don't spread any diseases in the village and please don't let any danger enter into our village.

Keep an eye over the enemies and injure them on the way before entering, to live safely and to be secured, to move freely and without any risks, you always have to help us.
Save us from the continuous rain, flood, drought.
Give us strength, stamina and courage to live happily.

2. Salutation to you, Mother *Jaher Era*.
On the occasion of the Baha festival, we offer you.
young fowls, new flowers, and freshly husked rice.
We beg of you to accept it with love and pleasure.
We pray to you :
We take these new flowers and fruits.
Let there be no disease and sickness from them.
When we are out in the forest hunting
please make the animals appear before us.

When our animals, the goats, the cows,
the cattle are grazing.
let them not be devoured by wild animals,
let the tigers leave them alone
and let them return home safe.
Let not disease and pestilence enter our village.
Bring us the rain-bearing clouds in time and with plenty
of rains let the earth be fresh and green.
And by quickening the mind and the body
bless everything with new life.

3. Our obeisance to you, Mother *Jaher Era*.
On the occasion of the *Erok* festival we offer to you.
Accept it in pleasure.
We pray to you :
For every seed we sow let there be twelve.

And let not disease attack them.
If they attack, please subdue them.
Do not allow weeds and grass to grow among our crops.
Do not allow diseases and misfortune to fall on our village.
Bring us the rain-bearing clouds in plenty.
Bring them in time.
Let the earth be green with our crops.
Let there be no hindrance to our movements.
Let there prevail among us
the spirit of mutual love and goodwill.

4. When the new leaves are coming in the sura plant.
At the time of plucking, digging and worshipping.
Salutation to you Mother *Jaher Era*.
On this occasion of '*Ma Mane*' we offer you young fowls, freshly husked rice.
Accept these wholeheartedly and with full satisfaction.
Let there be no disease and let no sickness enter our village.

Destroy or kill the wild animals on the way.
Destroy the contaminated wind and do not allow a single effect of it to fall on us.
Let the medicines have good effect on our people and everyone should be recovered from the dreaded diseases.
Bring us the rain-bearing clouds in plenty.
Bring them in time.
In our village, in our country, let there by happiness and goodwill all around.

5. Salutation to you mother Jaher Era.
On the occasion of threshing out of paddy grains from paddy sheaves, we offer you bunch of ears of paddy.
Accept it with full satisfaction and with clean heart.
We will also eat, chew them.

Don't allow us to have stomach pain and headache.
We will reap the ripe paddy plants at the paddy fields and store them in the paddy pits.
We will thresh the paddy by bullocks and winnow them after threshing.
Let there be little dust while winnowing.
Let there be plenty of paddy.
Let our houses be full of paddy.
Do not allow disease and misfortune to befall our village.
Make proper arrangements within the village for safe movements.
Let everyone be healthy and strong.
Let everyone grow well and live long.
Let everyone be blessed with true knowledge and wisdom.
(O; mother *Jaher Era*, convey our wishes to *Manek*, *Lita* and all other deities placed at *Jahera*).

6. *Dharam* (Bhagawan) all of your deeds are wonderful, mysterious and things of great use and enjoyment.

7. The stars and gods and all other ecclesiastical bodies are moving about in the heaven. The human beings and other living organisms living in the earth are watching the heavenly bodies.

8. The living beings are there to interpret these miraculous creations of the Almighty.

9. You are omnipresent and all things of your creation are always revolving around the universe.

10. Every thing that we observe in the sky and earth is revolving by your most powerful self and ever changing.

11. With good intention and also with bad intentions you are building up things as well as destroying them and vice versa.

12. In those days of yore all things were vanished and the heaven was void enveloped in darkness.

13. The light in its form of light and the darkness in its form of darkness were in existence in their respective spheres and were revolving constantly.

14. High above all these creations you are present in stillness enveloping all that you have created.

15. With so much power at your command you are in so much stillness that is appears that you are nonexistent.

16. You were also engulfed in the same illusions. The light

Translated from Bakhen composed by Pandit Raghunath Murmu in Santali language printed in OL CHIK script) and dark began to stay in a stage of meditation while merged in prayer addressed to you.

17. You started wishing to exhibit your wonderful power in order to let others come to know about you.

18. There was none at that time to have a glimpse of your presence and realize your divine powers.

19. You could not remain still. From the stillness you moved to a religious path.

20. In the guise of *Maranburu* you moved once towards right and in the guise of *Jahirain* you moved towards left and applied your power on these sides.

21. The divine powers were confronted with one another in the middle of the heaven. Cyclone accompanied by lightening and thunder over took the universe.

22. As a result of this revolution and rotation the sungod, stars, grahas and the universe itself were all born.

23. The sky and for that matter the heaven was lightened and out of the revolving motions you created everything and you yourself remained in these creations.

24. You kept the power of heat in the sun and the quality of coolness in the earth.

25. As a result of rotation of day and night the outer surface of earth got cooled and thereby air, soil, rock, water were originated.

26. The creator gave birth to two lives - *Hansa* and *Hanseli* who in their wandering got down on earth.

27. At that time there was no earth in the universe. The earth

was present at bottom above which there was water and at the top there was foam.

28. The female duck lay eggs on the foam and a large variety of living organisms were originated on the foam from water.

29. It was not possible for the soil to grow from the organisms. But the organisms developed divisiveness among themselves.

30. *Hingili*, the name of the earth rose up above water of the universe and was covered over by the *Pipili* (a covering).

31. *Hansa* and *Hanseli* flew up above the universe and thought of laying eggs on *Hingili* and *Pipili.*

32. The rock rose straight upwards and *Pipili* got white sand at its surface.

33. Thinking it as no good originating living organisms in the sand stone you developed distinctiveness in your creation.

34. The clouds rose up from water by the strength of air and there was rain over *Hingili* and *Pipili.*

35. The living Hansa and *Hanseli* rose up to the sky and came down on earth. They could not decide where to lay eggs.

36. By virtue of the distinctions that you created the earth rose up and grasses grew on *Hingili* and *Pipili.*

37. Hanseli lay egg on the grass and various types of living organisms grew at the place called *Pipili.*

38. You did not appreciate the birth of these varieties of

living organism, you wanted human beings to come up. Therefore you bestowed power for human beings to grow.

39. At *Pipili* the *Hanseli* lay eggs on the *Karama* tree which came up on the *Siram* grasses.

40. It was mysterious that the human babies came out of the eggs of *Hanseli*.

41. The babies cried and you heard their cries. "My mission will fulfilled, I thought, by their Cries", said the creator.

42. The works of *Hansa* and *Hanseli* are now over. The babies grew up under the shadow of yourself.

43. You brought down the babies and kept them among the living organisms.

44. In order to increase the number of human beings you gave one baby a name *Pilchu Halam* and the other one as *Pilchu Buddi*.

45. By the grace of yours both the *Pilchus* grew up and earned their livelihood following the ways you directed.

46. It may be due to the differences which you created among the living beings or due to some other reason the living beings took up different ways by which to earn their livelihood.

47. While going along the path of living in the world the *Pilchus* committed sin in the walks of their life and became waylaid.

48. You are kind and generous and advised them to follow the correct path.

49. Both the Pilchus strolled around *Hingli*. Surprisingly they could get from some source unknown to them a bow and an arrow and an axe.

50. In order to make their path of living clear they shot the arrow at the sky.

51. By virtue of your power the arrow fell straight on the ground and made a huge pit. The arrow fell on the ground in the beautiful *Jahera* of *Pipili*.

52. The *Pilchus* came to the *Jahera*. They appeared to be most joyful and happy. A heavenly feeling appeared in their mind.

53. You took birth in the heaven and *Pilchus* saw that you were ornamented with all kinds of power.

54. *Manek* and *Tureik* like your children were present on all sides as children do on all sides of their parents.

55. You had told *Pilchus* all that were needed for their existence.

56. The path for living peacefully was made clear and both the *Pilchus* praised you for everything that you did for them.

57. With the help of the arrow the path was made clear and this was established as what is called *Sarana Dharam*.

58. The almighty established the *Sarana Dharam* in the *jahera*. With the help of this religion *Pilchus* led their life comfortably and peacefully.

59. By the grace of the God *Pilchus* spent their days joyfully and were blessed with children.

60: You showered blessings on the children of *Pilchus*.

61. You created such human beings who had necessary qualities and bent of mind for recognizing your unlimited powers and greatness.

62. As desired by you the human beings were created but your wish for creation of such human beings remained unfulfilled.

63. You created divisions among the human beings by virtue of your skill and talents.

64. A persons does not get the taste of food when he is not hungry and a person does not realise what is good of good qualities if he has no experience of bad consequences resulting from evil deeds.

65. The creator created both good and bad qualities which exisit side by side and the man has to experience both these qualities in day to day life.

The Hill Kharias

Ethnographic Account

Identification, Origin and History

Simlipal hill ranges are the hearth and home of the Hill Kharias in Orissa. They are also found in insignificant number in the Manbhum, Chotanagpur and Singhbhum of Bihar, Midnapur and Bankura of Bengal, Balasore, Mayurbhanj, Keonjhar, Sambalpur and Dhenkanal of Orissa.

About the history of migration of the Hill Kharias, it is recorded that once they lived in the fertile river valley situated towards the north Vindhya and Kaimur range and with the advent of Aryans and annexation of other tribes, they moved up to the south of the hill ranges and subsequently settled in the hill ranges of Mayurbhanj district of Orissa. In course of time they spread into the hills of Singhbhum, Manbhum districts and other parts of Mayurbhanj district in Orissa. But ignoring this historical migration the Hill Kharias claimed themselves as the autochthons of the Mayurbhanj hills.

Dr. S.C. and R.C. Roy in their book 'The Kharias' has referred to Russel and his collaborator Rai Bahadur Hiralal, according to whom the etymology of the term Kharia is derived from *Kharkharia* which mean a palanquin or litter. The original name *Kharkharias* has been contracted to Kharias who carry palanquin. The Kharias are named so in accordance with the tradition that their first ancestors carried a *banghy* (carrying pole). The Kharia legend of origin resembles that of the Mundas, and tends to show that they are an elder branch of that tribe. The history of origin shows that their traditional occupation had been to till the soil and carry banghy. Besides, Dalton records the following tradition of origin "There is a tradition that the Kharias with another tribe called *Purans* were the aborigines of Mayurbhanj". They avow that they and the family of chief (*Bhanj*) were all produced from a pea-fowl's egg, the Bhanj from the yoke, the Purans from the white portion and the Kharias from the shell.

The Hill Kharias, who are most shy and conservative, keep themselves aloof from contact with other tribes and castes. They have adopted the speech of their Hindu neighbours. Among their present day neighbours, the Hill Kharias have such tribes as the Ho, the Santal and Caste Hindus. Thus inspite of their aloofness and exclusive habits, their contacts with other castes and tribes of their neighbours are not infrequent. The Hill Kharias have lost their own language and have adopted Oriya.

Nature of Settlement

The Hill Kharias live in the hills and forests of Mayurbhanj. Their villages vary in size from five families to twenty families or even more. They have no true villages. Groups of about four or five to a dozen or so families live together and form a settlement. A typical hill Kharia house is a small multipurpose rectangular hut with walls made of sal wood plastered with mud. The roof of the hut is made out of a double sloped wooden frame thatched with grass or straw. Ordinarily only one room is used by the Hill Kharia for both living or sleeping room and for cooking. In some houses, the only room is separated into two halves, one part for sleeping and the other part for cooking. The cooking is generally done on an open earthen oven, made by simply digging a hole in the ground. Dry wood is used as fuel.

Household Furniture and Articles

The household furniture, tools and appliances of the Hill Kharias include mats of date palm leaves, string cots, earthen vessels, gourd vessels, metal and silver utensils, bamboo baskets, leaf plates and cups, pestle and mortar, grinding stone, bow and arrow and axe and spear. During leisure time men make wooden artifacts such as pestles and mortars, bamboo sticks and bows, digging stick. They also make gourd ladles and drinking vessels and carrying poles.

Dress and Personal Adornment

The children remain naked till about five or six years of age, after which boys wear only a *Khadia*. This is a piece of loin cloth seven to ten inches in width and about one yard and a half in length. It is passed round the thigh and wound round the waist. This is worn till the age of about twelve. Adult men wear small dhotis and women wear white cotton sarees which fall upto the ankles. Now-a-days the advanced sections of the tribe are using modern dress. The Kharia women adorn themselves with various types of ornaments which include brass necklace, armlet, ear ring, finger ring and iron hair pin. Some young boys also use necklaces made of beads. Women use ribbons for adorning their hair.

Food

The main food of the Kharias include rice. Most Hill Kharias, however, do not grow rice themselves but procure it by barter from their neighbours. For the rest they have to depend occasionally on the spoils of the chase, and much more frequently on edible leaves, roots and fruits that they collect from the jungles, and some vegetables like beans, pumpkins, gourds, sweet potatoes, brinjals, cucumbers and the like which they grow in their kitchen garden. The Kharias, like other primitive tribes, are fond of rice beer called *Golang* in the Kharia language. *Golang* is also offered to the deities and spirits.

Hill Kharias are expert hunters using bows and arrows and sticks. They hunt almost all kinds of birds and animals. Fish does not form a regular article of food with them. They get rice by barter of honey which they collect skillfully. Honey serves as the medium of exchange.

Birth

Among the Hill Kharias after delivery the period of birth pollution is observed for nine days. The mother and the newly born baby take ceremonial bath on the ninth day. A few families observe a second purificatory ceremony on the 21st day after the child birth. During the purificatory ceremony a magico-religious rite is performed and the baby is given a name. The next noticeable event, is ear boring ceremony, which is held when the child is five or six years of age.

Marriage

Adult boys marry at the age of twenty and above and girls marry at the age of fifteen to eighteen years. They practise monogamy. Cross-cousin marriages are practised by them. Marriage by negotiation is the ideal pattern. The groom's party pays bride price. After marriage the couple establishes a neolocal residence. The other forms of marriage prevalent are, marriage by capture, elopement and service. In their society divorce is allowed and widows are permitted to remarry.

Among the Hill Kharias the payment of the bride price constitutes a ceremony. On the appointed day, the boy's parents with about half a dozen relatives and friends go to the girl's house. There their legs and feet are anointed with turmeric paste and washed; mats are spread out for them to sit and they are given powdered tobacco and lime to refresh themselves with. Relatives and friends of the bride's parents assemble. Then a mimic bargaining, enlivened by would be sister-in-law of wit and fun, the Bride price is paid. The bride price is usually fixed according to circumstances. Besides money, a *sari* (cloth) and some ornaments for the bride are given. The boy's parents have also to present a *sari* (cloth) to the bride's mother.

No particular ceremony or formalities are required for the fixing the date of marriage. The month of *Magh* (January-Feburary) is the season for a Hill Kharia marrige, but marriages can be held in the month of *Phalgun* (February-March). Any day of the week except a Sunday or a Saturday or a Thursday may be chosen to celebrate the marriage. Should it, however, be fixed on a Thursday, the bride may on no account leave her parents' house on that day. This ban on Thursday is obviously due to the influence of Hindu ideas.

Death

Ordinarily the dead of a Hill Kharia receives an earth burial. Only a few well to do families practise cremation. But those died of leprosy, small-pox and cholera are burnt. Similarly those who died by snake-bite, by falling from a tree or hill, or other forms of unnatural death meet the same fate.

When the burial or cremation is finished, all who attend it purify themselves by taking a bath and go to the house of the deceased with their wet clothes on. There they sit down for a while and spend the time in smoking. Death pollution lasts for ten days. Those who are polluted are forbidden to eat fish or flesh, nor shave, or pare their nails. On the tenth day, all the members of the family get themselves shaved, their hair is clipped and their nails pared by a fellow tribe's man. After a purificatory bath a funeral feast is provided to relatives and fellow tribals. This communal meal is known as "*Shudha-bhat*" or "purifying-meal".

Social Organisation and the Regulation of Tribal Life :

The smallest social unit is the family which is elementary consisting of parents and their children. A Kharia family centres round the father through whom lineage or descent is traced and who exercises authority in the family. In few cases, the Hill Kharia family includes an adopted son or a son-in-law. The son after being married builds a separate hut for himself and lives with his wife and children.

Ownership of family property ordinarily vests with men. A Kharia woman, after her marriage, lives in her husband's house. A Kharia husband though exercises more or less general authority over his wife, the latter exercises considerable influence over her children and household affairs and has a voice in matters of domestic economy. Her influence over her husband is by no means negligible.

The Hill Kharias of Mayurbhanj have practically no clan organisation at the present day. If they had any in the past they have forgotten it. Some Kharias refer to Cobra (*Nag*) as their clan. But it is borrowed from the neighbouring hindus.

Among the Hill Kharias, each settlement acknowledges the priest as the leaders in social as well as religious matters. The priest is generally senior most member of the settlement. He is called as the *Dehuri* or *Dihuri* among the Hill Kharias and takes decision in matters concerning the settlement in consultation with the heads of the families.

The traditional political organisation of the Kharias is constituted at two different levels, one at the village level and the other at the inter village level, to keep the solidarity and law and order intact. The Hill Kharias have a Panchayat of their own headed by Pradhan. Cases regarding breach of any taboo and disputes about partition, divorce, adultery and the like are decided in the meeting of the village council. The village council raises funds for public worship, religious feasts and for sacrifice at the time of epidemic. The members of the council remain present in rites and ceremonies relating to birth, marriage and death. In case of serious offences the village council has the power to excommunicate a person from the society. Above the village council there exists the inter village council which they call *Bhira*. Among the Hill Kharias the *Bhira* consists of representatives of some inter-linked settlements and is headed by the eldest, wisest and most influential Pradhan of these settlements.

Now-a-days, modern panchayat system has been introduced in Kharia areas. But it is not fully effective as the people are not educated. They are guided by their traditional village council.

Religious Practices and Belief System

The Hill Kharias, have unlike other tribal groups, comparatively fewer deities and spirits in their pantheon, and have much less elaborate rites and ceremonies. Their public festivals in which the village priest conducts the religious rites are connected mostly with hunting. Dharam or the supreme deity is first invoked and then the *Isti Pat* or the tutelary hill spirit of the village including all other *pats* or hill spirits are worshipped. The village deity or Gram devata called Baram is also worshipped. Baram is invoked and propitiated as a jungle spirit by all sections, of the Hill Kharias. They also pay respect to the God of fire. Along with these deities they also worship the deities like Durga, Kali, Shiva, Parvati and other Hindu gods and goddesses. Before going to the forest they offer puja to the *Banadurga* (forest goddess) for good luck.

Religious practices are bound up with the Kharias economic pursuits. In fact most of the periodical religious rites and festivals of the tribe are intended to bring good luck in their economic pursuits. Before the Kharia goes out on a hunting expedition and again on return after a successful hunt, and when he has collected honey and before he begins sowing or harvesting his crops and while eating the first fruits of his fields, the blessings of the deities and spirits who are believed to control nature must be invoked for better results and good luck.

The Hill Kharias have different festivals. There is a saying that they have thirteen festivals in twelve months. Makar Sankranti and Raja Sankranti are the major festivals. They observe these festivals by singing songs in accompaniment of music.

Economic Life

The Hill Kharia livelihood is based on hunting and food gathering. Among these Kharias the men do the hunting and women do the gathering of fruits and tubers, edible leaves and herbs although men also do gathering and dig tubers when no food is available by hunting or fishing.

The Hill Kharias are expert tree climbers. They collect honey and wax, which they sell for cash. They are expert in honey collection. It is on a dark night that the Hill Kharias apply smoke to the hives, by which the bees fly away. Then on the following morning they collect the hives in a vessel and extract the honey. The hives are generally on the precipitous sides of the hills which can not be reached on foot. So a ladder is made by twisting the fibres of siali creepers holding the cross bars of bamboo with which to climb up to dislodge the hives.

It is interesting to note that the Hill Kharias of the Similipal hills (Mayurbhanj) have divided the forests and hills in several portions which they call *Bhandar* (store house). The right to collect honey in a particular *Bhandar* is recognised by them to belong to particular families and no one else thinks of encroaching upon another's *Bhandar* for collecting honey. Every family does not 'own' such a *Bhandar*, but some one having no *Bhandar* can collect in another's *Bhandar* with the owner's permission.

Living more or less isolated in their inhospitable hill fastness of Mayurbhanj the Hill Kharias have always had to carry on a strenuous struggle for bare existence. They mostly depend upon food gathering and hunting which are their major source of income. Their forest collections include resin, wax, honey, tasar cocoons, gum and lac, tapioca etc. They barter the forest produce for paddy and other cereals.

In the Mayurbhanj hills, the Kharias, who have any *jhum* or *Dahi* cultivation, work on their fields during the agricultural season and those who have no land either work as day labourers or go out in search of labour. From May to July, they collect honey and bee-wax and catch birds, particularly the species called *Sari/Sua* or *Maina* which they sell or barter. Men and women gather the corolla of *Mahul* (*Bassia latifolia*). They carry bows and arrows and axes while going to the jungles. A few Kharias are experts in killing tigers with their long bows and arrows. In recent past some of the Hill Kharias have left their hill dwellings and moved up to other parts of the area in

search of livelihood. Now they are living with peasant communities in the plains. This contact with caste Hindus has brought some noticeable changes in their techno-economic and religious life. As a result, they have taken up settled agriculture, animal husbandry and wage earning for their livelihood.

FOLKLORE OF THE HILL KHARIAS

In spite of this strenuous existence the Hill Kharias relax when they get leisure. This is the time when they sit with their elders i.e. grand parents, and old persons to listen to many stories and worldly events. The old men, at the moments of leisure, impart their traditional knowledge and ideas in the form of folk tales and myths and the knowledge and wisdom based on observation and experience of generations. Besides, dancing and singing are the main source of amusement. Young men and women among them enjoy themselves in an evening and on festive seasons by singing and dancing and playing on the *changu* or the *madal* drums. Many of the songs of the Hill Kharias, relate to the Hindu god Krishna or Hari and other Hindu gods. Their arduous annual round of activities are forgotten on occasions of seasonal religious feasts and festivals.

Some of the stories and songs which are part of the folklore of the Hill Kharias of Mayurbhanj are mentioned below.

STORIES

The Goat Boy and the Princes

In the forest a Kharia couple lived with their children. The couple used to collect resin, mushroom, honey etc. from the jungle. One day they had gone to the forest with their youngest child where they found a creeper of bitter potato. They immediately started digging that spot to take out the bitter potato. At last they found so many potatoes that it was impossible for them to carry the child back home.

So they left him near a bush and returned home with the bitter potatoes.

After some time the boy started crying which was heard by a tiger and a tigress. So they followed the cry and reached the child. The tigress being sympathetic towards the child took him to her house instead of making him her prey. Gradually the child started growing by taking tigress milk. He also wandered about in the forest and collected forest fruits and used to bring food for the tiger and tigress. When he started hunting wild animals, the tiger became apprehensive and told the tigress that he could also be dangerous for them and so they should eat him quickly. The tigress felt sorry at the tiger's attitude as it was difficult for her to think in such a manner about the child whom she gave all her love and care and brought him up to this age. But the tiger being very strict in his decision fixed up the day to eat the boy and invited the other tigers of the jungle to accompany him. As the day of death came closer, the tigress became sorrowful. The tigress reported the plot to the boy, hearing which the boy replied back, 'mother please do not worry about me, I can take care of myself' - On the day of the planned murder the boy went into the forest in the morning taking along his bow and arrow. He climbed up a huge Sal tree and sat at the top. He had told the tigress to follow him and to stay somewhere near him. After sometime all the tigers of the forest assembled there and without finding the boy started grumbling over the tiger for cheating them. The tiger got furious and tried to kill the tigress. The tigress said that the boy had gone to the jungle for hunting and he could get him if he would go to the forest. Accordingly all of them went to the forest and saw him at the top of a huge sal tree. They sought for ways to kill the boy.

At last, they came to the conclusion that they would climb the tree and catch the boy. They made a ladder for this purpose. The tigress stayed at the base of the ladder and all others climbed up and at the top of the ladder was the tiger who tried to pull the boy out from the tree. The boy immediately started shooting his arrows at the tigers and killed them one by one. As a result, all the tigers were killed except the tigress who fled into the forest. The boy followed her and found a pond full of lotus flowers. A girl was trying to pluck one lotus and as she approached the flower, the flower moved away. Finally, the girl requested the Kharia boy to pluck the flower for her. The boy asked her what would she give him if he would bring her the flower. The girl replied whatever he wanted she would give him. The boy again asked "would you marry me" to which the girl readily agreed. On this bargain the boy agreed to get the lotus and thus he got into the pond and brought the beautiful lotus for her, The girl was delighted and agreed to marry the boy. She went to call the washerman and barber to clean the boy as he was looking very untidy with long hair and long nails. She explained everything to the barber and sent him to the place where the pond is located. The girl then went to her house to get the dress. But the barber planned that he could marry the girl after killing the boy on the plea of making him clean. He came near the pond, and while cutting his hair he cut the head of the boy and threw it into the pond. When the girl came and without finding the boy asked the barber. The barber said that the boy had again gone to the jungle. The girl being suspicious became furious and cursed the barber that his wishes would never be fulfilled and he would roam around the forest throughout his life. Thus all the wishes of the barber were shattered. The girl went back home in despair. Again as usual when on the next day she went to the pond to take bath, she found only one lotus was present in the middle of the pond. The moment she touched the flower, it came to the edge of the pond. At last, she plucked the flower and went back home. She wore it in her hair and dressed up. The moment she wore the flower her head started reeling and she felt dizzy. She threw that lotus into the garbage where gradually a plant grew. She took the green leaves and cooked them. While cooking she heard a noise coming out of those leaves. "Tak Tak Barber, Tak Tak Barber". The girl got scared and threw it into the garden. There again an orange plant grew and fruits came out within a short time. The girl used to sleep under the tree everyday and the leaves used to fall on her. Once when she was sleeping one fruit fell and rolled over. One goat rearer took that fruit to his house. He gave that fruit to his mother and told that he has brought it from king's palace which the king had thrown out. His mother then went to cut that fruit and immediately she heard a voice, "please do not cut it in the middle but from only both sides". His mother did so. From the middle of the fruit a boy came out and the goat owner got very pleased as he had no brother. He told that "we will go to the jungle together for feeding the goats". The boy gradually grew. They started rearing more and more goats. The boy became expert in the art of archery and his courage astonished everyone. Once the king invited kings and princes for the marriage of his daughter. The princess had a condition and the one who would fulfil it would marry her. So all the kings tried to hit the target but in vain. This boy was also present there who successfully hit the target and married the princess. This goat grazier was that Kharia boy who became the flower first, then a small plant, then an orange plant and lastly got his body back from the fruit.

The Jackal and the Deaf Old Man

Once upon a time in a forest there lived a deaf old man with his blind wife. They had a small piece of land to cultivate which was their only source of livelihood. One after noon, the old man had gone to plough the land. The route from his house to his land was marked by him which was daily followed by his blind wife for taking his food to the field. One day a jackal imitating the old man's voice deceived the old woman and ate the food meant for the old man. This mischief was repeated by the jackal for a number of times which annoyed the old man and he quarrelled with his wife. The old woman also retaliated stating thereby, "oh old man, everyday you are eating and also scolding me, if you do not want to keep me tell me directly so that I can go to my father's house. Hearing this the old man came to the conclusion that really the old woman was taking food for him but somebody is eating the same on the way. Once he hid himself and saw that one shrewd jackal was eating the food. He thought of taking revenge on the jackal and continued to take his own rice to the field. After seeing this the shrewd jackal, said, "hey deaf old man, I will eat all the corn from your field". To retaliate, on the corn field the old man prepared a fire and slept nearby covering himself with dust. When the jackal came to the field the old man hit him with a stick. The shrewd jackal thought to take revenge by giving a blow to the old man and told the old man accordingly.

The old man thought of taking revenge once again and was thinking of killing the shrewd jackal. As per his plan he informed his wife to invite all the jackals for eating his dead body. The old woman went to the forest crying and repeating about the invitation of the old man's death feast. All the jackals along with the shrewd jackal reached the old man's place tor the same and seeing them the old woman started crying. When the jackals tried to console her she stopped crying and started tying them with a rope. When they enquired about the same, she stated that it was their custom to give food only after tying with rope. Then she called her husband to hit all the jackals once each with the stick and to hit the shrewd jackal five times. The old man followed the same which resulted in the death of the shrewd jackal and all other jackals ran into the forest. From that day onwards the jackals are afraid of human beings.

The Old Demoness

Once upon a time in a village there lived one old demoness with her grand daughter. Being afraid of her all the villagers used to give them food in turn. If she was dissatisfied with anybody's food, she used to eat his cattle by boiling them in water.

She had a large body and had eyes like saucers. Her nails were big and sharp and hair hung upto her feet. She surreptitiously used to eat all the goats of the village. In the same village a poor cattle rearer also lived. Oneday his turn came to supply food for the demoness. But he didn't have anything even for himself to eat and did not know what to do. The demoness after reaching his place became furious without finding anything to eat, and tied him up in a sack. She then carried him along with her. On the way back she became thirsty for which she stayed near a pond to drink water. In the meantime the cattle rearer came out of the sack and filled it with stones and thorns and left the place. Coming back from the pond the demoness picked up the sack and started moving. But on the way the stones gave her a lot of pain reacting to which the demoness scolded the cattle rearer addressing, "you fool, you are hitting me with your knee and I will first break those and eat them". As the thorns pricked her, she thought that the cattle rearer was doing so. She threatened, "I will also eat your fingers by cutting them". After reaching her house the demoness told her grand

daughter "today I have brought some good food, cook it quickly". The grand daughter being afraid put water in a vessel and made preparation for cooking. But when she poured the contents of the sack into the vessel, the vessel broke. Seeing this the demoness being outraged for being cheated by the cattle rearer and out of hunger chased her grand daughter to eat. But the grand daughter being well aware of the habits of her grandmother had already hidden herself and informed the villagers regarding the matter. The villagers came to her rescue and unitedly killed the demoness. At last the cattle rearer returned to the village by marrying the grand daughter.

Father

Once upon a time a king ruled over a kingdom. He had two daughters whom he loved immensely. Once he called both his daughters and asked them, "how much you love me". The elder daughter replied, "father : I love you like salt". The younger daughter said, "I love you like sugar". He felt offended with the reply of the elder daughter, and decided to get her married to a beggar. Accordingly a young beggar was searched for and finally the elder daughter was given in marriage to a beggar for which she became unhappy and left her father's place with her husband. After going to a far off place they purchased some land where they built a house and started cultivation. Her husband used to till the land and sell the produce in the local market. Their hard labour, gradually made them rich and they lived like kings. Being aware of this the king came to see his daughter. His daughter treated him well and served him mutton curry along with other curries for lunch. While eating, the daughter asked, "father, which curry you liked the most". The king replied, "all the curries are good except the mutton curry in which you have forgotten to put salt". Immediately she replaced that mutton curry with another plate of mutton curry with salt which tasted good. Simultaneously she reminded her father, "father when you had asked us how much we loved you, in reply I had stated that I loved you like salt which implied my intense love for you. The curry becomes tasteless without salt. Similarly my life has no meaning without you. The king understood the depth of knowledge of his elder daughter and repented. He distributed the kingdom between the two daughters and directed the elder daughter to be the queen and left the kingdom.

Tiger and Super Tiger

In a forest there lived a tiger in a cave. All the goats of the village went to that forest to graze. As the forest was very dense a wooden bell was tied on the neck of each goat the sound of which helped their owner to track them out of forest. Once being afraid of a heavy storm the goat owner came back home alone leaving them in the forest. As a result the goats became helter and skelter and returned to the house except biggest one. The goat owner thought that most probably the tiger had eaten that goat and therefore decided that he would call the villagers in the morning to kill the tiger.

On the other side the goat in the forest reached the tiger's cave and stayed there. The tiger after returning to the cave heard the sound of the wooden bell and being scared asked from outside; "who are you" ? The goat in reply asked "who are you" ? The tiger replied, "I am tiger". The goat replied "I am super tiger". Being afraid the tiger requested, O brother!

this is my house, please leave it. "On the other hand the goat being afraid was coming out of the cave. But the tiger seeing his horn and hearing the sound of the wooden bell ran away. On the way he found a jackal who asked "Oh uncle where are you going ?" The tiger hesitatingly replied "What to do nephew ? A super tiger is living in my house and is chasing me". The jackal being sympathetic assured the tiger. "Oh uncle ! do not worry, as long as I am there nobody can eat you". Finally both the tiger and the jackal tied tails together and hesitantly returned to the cave. After reaching there they repeated the same question enquiring about the goat. In reply the goat also repeated his question. When the tiger said that he is tiger, the goat said I am a super tiger and started running outside. Scared by the sound of the wooden bell both the jackal and the tiger ran away. The goat on the other hand returned to his owner's house.

Ujjal Singh

Once upon a time there lived a poor man named Ujjal Singh. Most of the days he was sleeping without any food. The

people who know him neither gave him any work nor helped him getting his food. For this reason he was living a depressed life. In such a situation he left that place and reached a nice gentleman's house. He was sympathetic towards Ujjal Singh and appointed him in his work for one year. In the beginning Ujjal Singh did all the works perfectly. Once the owner sent him to sow paddy in the field. Ujjal Singh, instead of sowing paddy in the field, spread chaffs in the field. As a result no paddy plant came up. When his owner enquired about the same he replied that he had sown paddy. But when his owner asked him to show the sample of the paddy, he showed the chaffs. Seeing this the owner could know that he was an ignorant person and therefore there would be a huge loss. Thereafter he drove Ujjal Singh out from the job. On the way back Ujjal Singh climbed a tree and started cutting the same branch, on which he was sitting. A Brahmin was passing by who saw him and said, "you fool : you will fall down. After sometime when he really fell down from the tree he thought the brahmin must be a big astrologer and therefore he followed the brahmin and asked him to tell him the date of his death. The brahmin said, "the day on which you will see stars while sleeping in your house will be your last day". So when once due to strong wind the roof of his house was blown away, and the stars became

visible. Ujjal Singh saw them. He thought that he had died and slept like a dead person. The villagers took him to the cremation ground. While putting him on the pyre he ran away. The villagers thought him to be a ghost and killed him.

SONGS

The Hill Kharias of Mayurbhanj have no specific language. They speak Oriya. Most of their songs and stories are in Oriya language. They sing some songs in their mother tongue. Although they sing different songs on different occasions *Raja*, and *Makar Sankranti* are the most important ones. During *Raja* festival they sing cradle songs (*Doli* song) and on the occasion of *Makar Sankranti* they sing cradle songs (*changu* song). Most Kharia songs are meant to be sung at the seasonal dances. Only a few of them are not accompanied by dancing. Most of their marriage songs are called "*Durang*". Besides, some songs are sung when they are involved in their games. Some songs are included in a few folktales and some are chanted by their magicians while practising magic.

The subject matter of the Kharia songs relates to love and joy and sorrows of lovers. A joyful appreciation of the beauty of flowers and birds would be marked in a large number of Kharia songs. The songs reveal the real soul of the tribe, perhaps even more directly than their customs and institutions do. In order to enter into the spirit of the songs and of the singers, one has to hear the songs sung with their usual accompaniment of dance and music in the natural surroundings. The songs of the Hill Kharias are divided into the following types :-

1. Marriage songs - At each stage of a marriage they sing different songs.
2. *Doli* songs - Doli songs are sung during the festival of *Raja*. The boys and girls sing this song sitting on the swing made of *siali* plant.
3. *Changu* song - The boys and girls while dancing sing this *changu* song. They dance with steps according to the different lyrics of a song.

4. *Jhumer* — These are sung on the occasion of *Karma*. This is a mixture of both Oriya and Bengali language. Karama festival is not the festival of Kharias. They have borrowed it from their neighbouring communities.

MARRIAGE SONG

1. Bela Ta Tiki Parita Dau Dau
Asai Balaku Bandai, Ghurijare Bela,
Pheri Jare Bali Ke Bajiba Tarasa.

Meaning

It is the time of dawn and the sun is rising in the sky. The bride like a fairy is looking more beautiful at this moment and is glittering with the sunrays. The sun rays are also compared with the groom. Go back, turn back and the sun rays will fall on the bride.

2. *Tentuli Mula Re Dhana Bunili,*
Paria Raja Khaila, Ghuri Pheri
Paria Raja Ye Phansa.
Dali Paria Raja Khaila, Ghuri
Pheri, Barara Bapo Boli Na Janajen,
Marideli Khandia Khabal Hata
Deviti Pakei Deli, Hasile Disai Gala.

Meaning

(Here bride's house is being compared with the paddy field and the groom's party is with the *Paria raja*). When the groom is coming to the bride's house to take her it is said - he has come to eat paddy from the field.

3. *Bali Jie Mukuta Tiari Kare, Se Bali*
Mukuta Ba Bana Kukuta Dhari Thae
Kintu Gala Ba Kantha Ku Labanga
Aram Die

Meaning

One who is worshipping his sacred thread utters these

words. He is actually a bastard, not a pious person dedicating his life to worship.

4. *Bahare Asuka Kodi, Mote Lagauachi Jama Daudi, Mo Jiba Jaukhi Chadi, Mo Jiba Jibale Bele, Katha Duikhanda, Ani Bandhile Masanu Padaku Nele, Masani Padaku Nei, Gata Kudi, Mati Dhankai Padaku Nei, Gata Kudi, Mati Dhankai Dei, Kandhuchanti Bapa Bhal, Bapalhai Bada Mitha, Gadhi Mundi Kari Khaila Pita Bapaku Lagila Chinta*

Meaning

The sound of conch is heard from outside. My life is going to remain in the abode of yama. I am going to die, I am in my last stage, bring two logs of wood and tie them. Take me to the cremation ground. Dig a hole to put me inside and sprinkle mud over it. Parents are mourning. Its a song of the bride while leaving the house of her parents.

DOLL SONGS

1. *Nadia Khini Kuri, Mote Chadi Kanta*
Jaulhi Puri, Gala Re Deija Churi,
Kahiki Debi Mun Churi, Pancha Barsha
Hele Asibi Pheri, Rahithiba Deha Dhari

Meaning :

The wife is telling her husband 'I ate the grated coconut, my husband is going to Puri leaving me, strangle me and then go.

Husband :

Why should I strangle you. I will come back after five years. You stay with your body.

2. *Kuade Jaucha Asa, Chuda Chari*
Mana, Nadia Rasa, Eithere Danta Ghasa.

Meaning :

Where are you going ? Come here, bring flat rice and coconut milk and wash your teeth.

3. *Kahien Haucha Bichehu,*
Asa Mo Sangata Re Dekhai
Debi Kete Sile Mara Chhabi

Meaning

Why are you so worried ? Oh my friend ! come I will show you many cinemas.

4. *Eka Bahulia Doli, Dui Bahulia Khajuri*
Koli, Sita Khauchanti Toli.
Sitanku Kuita Uttara, Ki Dukha Padila
Sita Tora, Mun Kahe Apsara.

Meaning

One armed swing two armed dates.
Ask Sita what sorrow she has.
The sages and heavenly nymphs are asking.

5. *Banaste Dakila Picha*
Aji Nani Mane Pahali Raja.
Kiniana Sajabaja

Meaning

A bird sings in the forest, "Today is the first day of the festival "*Raja*". So bring the dressing items.

Jhumer

1. *Amba Phale Junka Tunka,*
Tentuli Phale Banka Banka, Tumara
Deshare Aieli Randi Hate Re Sankha
Ki Kahibi Loka Naje Mun Padibi
Dagebaji

Meaning

Mangoes are round and round
Tamarinds are in bunch
Saw a widow wearing bangles
at your place.
What will I say in embarrassment.

2. *Upara Ta Chand Guru Mule Go,*
Tata Bali Tata Bali Kake Kibi
Harmar Bapa Boli.

Meaning

At the upperside is moon god, at the lower side is hot sand. Whom should I call my father.

3. *Am Pakka Jeman Teman, Tentuli Pakka*
Bhala, Tentuli Rasa Dnani, Mora, Bela
Pakka Bhala.

Meaning

Mangoes are ripe, tamarind is ripe
Tamarind juice : you are mine

4. *Chaiti Baishakha Mase, Kanta Baisa,*
Chamar Ba Se.
Bujhi Niago Jagate Sangarl, AR
Ki Rahiba Bapa Ghare.

Meaning

In the summer season the black bees bore into the bamboo and bush trees.
Understand the universe and the rules of the society.
No more will you stay at your parents house.

5. *Hatke Jabar Bela, Chaila Kani Che Jala*
Ego Gunamani, E Sunamani Sajabela
Bojha Buhe Bada Bhari Lage

Meaning

While going to the weekly market, the children disturb. Oh, my darling wife : it is difficult to carry loads in the evening.

CHANGU SONG

1. Pachila Kadamba Koli Phale Dale Dale
Pachi Padijiba Jale Lo Rasabiti
Tora Lagi Amali Jibana.

Meaning

The fruit of Kadamba is ripe in the different branches of the tree. It will fall down, oh my darling. For you this is life and for you it will disappear.

2. Satmat Bandhibe Tata Tickata
Katibe, Rele Basi Tandia Be Mor Ar
N Rahiba E Khane

Meaning

Pack your luggage soon. Book the ticket for Tata and show the flag sitting in the train. I will not stay here.

3. Gacha Madhye Tulasi,
Patara Madhye Panare,
Chiri Madhye Radhika Sundari
He Bhagaban.

Meaning

Among the plants, Tulsi,
Among the leaves, Pan.
Among the women, Radhi
Beautiful. Oh ! my God.

4. *Tume Jadi Hamar-Het Bhal Bhal Go*
Sali Neta, Sali Chadi Jakit Kina I deba
Tora Jakit Tora Ke Sajab.

Meaning

If you will become mine, you will get beautiful sarees. You will buy blouses to match sarees. Your blouse will look beautiful in your body.

5. *Ata Go Hamar, Pitha Amake Nha*
Go Deli, Adin Tentuli Go Antare
Chenka Hail.

Meaning

Flour is mine, you did not give me flour cake. In the mean time tamarind became sour in my mind.

The Kharia's love of flowers
(Kharia song P. 484 'The Kharias')

1. *Pokeraya hiro-te jongor jongor ra'ra' ;*
Re yota yota jiyom gebta, hare hae, Daiya !
Re yota yota jiyom gebta, hare hae, Daiya !
Dhae se re konon babu, kej olem re.
Yota yota jiyom malata, hare hare, Daiya !
Yota yota jiyom malata, hare hare Daiya.

Meaning

This songs describes the joy of a Kharia girl when she looks at the lovely red flowers blooming on the bank of a tank. The girl tells her younger brother to bring those flowers for her.

The Kharia's love of birds
(Kharia song P. 488 'The Kharias')

1. *Banklui ki Babu, Rajaleke kachhari taki.*
Raja-leke kachhari taki.
Bainsi toblungte raja-leke kachhari taki.
Raja leke kachhari taki.

Meaning

In this song, the herons (one type of birds) are compared with kings. When a heron sits on the back of a buffalo, it looks like a king sitting on his throne.

Affection between brothers and sisters
(Kharia song P. 493 'The Kharias')

1. *Ingko ingko, Dada, kosor laro juentu te,*
Uminga ro' dokona ?
Ingko ingko, Dada, khatia machia te dokonaing.,

Khatia machiate dokonaing.
Ingko ingko, Dada, kosor kondeng
Kanasibung umingaro kade.
Uminga ro kade
Ingko ingko Dada bon-bhainsa derenga,
Kanasibung kading,
Kanasibung ului kading.

Meaning

In this song, a sister eulogizes on her brother because he provides luxuries to her. She appeals to him to provide stringed cots and stringed stools in stead of palm-leaf mats in which she wants to sit, and buffalo-horn combs instead of bamboo combs by which she wants to comb her hair.

A song expressing love between young men and women (Kharia song P. 499 'The Kharias')

1. *Changda-no godjhung te ber rutu pedte ?*
Ber rutu pedte re ?
Durit belong konsel, da olna cholta
Romod-da gurta, Romod-la gurta.
Dhain-se, re Bhai joe ! Mate gamgorem,
Apa-te utun-gorem, Ing uming chona,
Hae inya Ma joe, bhainsi-no obsongore,
Kongtang-no obsongore, Ing uming chona.

Meaning

This song narrates the attraction of a beautiful Kharia girl towards a young boy who plays bamboo flute on her way to the village-stream. Her beauty is compared with a sweet fruit. She tells her brother to inform their parents regarding her intention to marry that young man. She wants to get married by any means and therefore suggests her mother to sell their cattle and pay the bride price for her marriage.

A Song Expressing Love for Hunting

(Kharia song P. 503 'The Kharias')

1. *Kuda golang bingoe bongoe,*
Gudlu golang bingoe-bongoe.
Ani Dada, re sikaro chona.
Dada joe ani nanare sikaro chona.
Khajartarte kondej bung go'te;
Litia tarte, dang-bung go'te;
Ani-Nana-re sikaro chona.
Bhaiare, ani Dada re, sikaro chona.

Meaning

This song gives description about Kharia's hunting experience. The singer is inspired by the sweet taste of millet beer and gudlu-beer which he drinks before going out on a hunting trip. He calls out his fellow men and women to join him and bring home the games and birds with the helps of long sticks or hatchet-handles.

The Oraons

Ethnographic Account

Identification, Origin and History

The Oraons are one of the major tribes in the country. They have been listed as Scheduled Tribes in West Bengal, Bihar, Orissa, Madhya Pradesh and Maharashtra. In Orissa the Oraon population constitutes 3.64 per cent of the state's total tribal population. They are mainly concentrated in the district of Sundergarh and Sambalpur and adjoining areas of Bihar and Madhya Pradesh. Numerically the Oraons constitute the largest tribe of the district of Sundergarh.

According to Oraon tradition, their original homeland is said to be in Deccan. Roy (1915) has made an attempt to reconstruct the Oraon history prior to their entry into the present habitat of Chotanagpur. When they entered the Chotanagpur plateau, they found the area occupied by tribes who are economically more backward than themselves. The Kora and Birhor till then were either hunters or herdsmen. The Mundas who had taken to agriculture, followed a very rudimentary method of tilling the soil. Here they settled down but could not give up the habit of moving from one place to another under hard economic pressure in search of suitable patches of land for cultivation for their livelihood. Some of them migrated to Orissa and some others to Madhya Pradesh.

There are several folktales relating to the origin of the community and their name was cited by early ethnologists, particularly S.C. Roy (1915). The Oraons in their own language call themselves *Karukh*. The origin of this name is sometimes traced back to one of their mythical hero king called *Karakh*. To this personage tradition ascribes the origin of the ancient name *Karus-Desh* which roughly comprised what is now the district of Shahabad. Although the name of the country as *Karukh-Desh* is now lost, the memory of their past days under their ancient king *Karukh* has not been perhaps forgotten by the Oraons. The name *Karukh* was probably derived originally from obsolete Dravidian root meaning 'Man' and it might have been given to the mythical king *Karukh* just in the same way as the name Adam was given to the Hebrew Progenitor of Mankind.

Since the first parents of the community were born from the blood of the chest (*Uras* or *Ur* in Sanskrit) of the holy ascetic, they were first known as *Urager*, *Thakur* and then as Oraon for their unholy and unclean food habit.

According to another folktale they had connection with one of the ancient kings' *Karakh* and sometimes they were commonly known as *Karukh*. However, the tribe and their original mother tongue are still known as *Karukh* although they are commonly referred to as Oraon or Dhangara.

They have their own language called Kurukh which is classified as Dravidian language. Those who inhabit the border areas of Bihar, speak *Sadri* which is a mixture of Hindi and several tribal dialects of Chotanagpur plateau.

Nature of Settlement

Although they live in mixed villages, they tend to build separate settlements of their own. In the past each family had a tendency to build its house close to its reclaimed agricultural land. But now the Oraon settlements barring a few in the interior areas bordering Madhya Pradesh, are established without following any definite plan. Houses in a settlement are usually scattered and connected with uneven and irregular lanes. They now build spacious houses with fire-proof roof of *Naria* tiles (*khappar*) in place of small houses with wild grass thatched roof. Majority of houses are found with mud walls and two sloped naria tile roof opened to courtyard. These houses have high verandah at the back and low verandah in front. Houses are generally not constructed facing the village lane. Most of the houses have more than one living room, the number of which depends upon the size of the family. The cowshed or pigsty are built close to living room.

Household Furniture and Articles

The household articles include *Khattia* (*Charpoy*) and mat made of date-palm leaves which are used as bed. Well-to-do families have wooden and steel chairs, wooden tables and cots and steel and wooden almirahs. Plates and cups made of brass and bell metal for taking food, earthen and aluminum pots for cooking food and earthen vessels for storing water, bamboo baskets of different sizes and shapes are common household articles. The gourd-bottle for carrying rice and rice beer is very fast disappearing and the aluminium tiffin carrier is becoming popular in its place. Agricultural, fishing and hunting implements possessed by them are quite similar to those seen in the households of the neighbouring Hindus. Modern articles like bicycles, lantern, suitcase, steel trunk, cotton umbrella, radio, tape recorder etc. are found in many households.

Dress and Personal Adornment

The traditional dress of the Oraon is *Kareya* for male and *Khanria* for female which are woven in self-made yarn by a weaving caste called *Ganda*. Now-a-days, there clothes are being replaced by modern sarees and other dresses available in the local market. A limited variety of ornaments made of gold, silver and alloys are used by women. Tattoo marks are usually seen among the old women.

Food

The staple food of the Oraons is rice which is occasionally supplemented by gruel of millet. They have changed their food habits after coming in contact with the neighbouring Hindus. They are no more omnivorous as in the past. They have given up many items which are considered unclean by the local people. They relish the meat of goat, pig and fowl. Non-vegetarian food and cakes constitute the festive dishes on ceremonial occasions. Rice beer which they brew, *mahua* liquor and tobacco smoking and tobacco chewing are their traditional use of intoxication. However, the use of *gudakhu* (tobacco paste) has become more popular among their women in present time.

Birth

The birth pollution continues for 7 to 10 days when the *chhati* (purification rite) is observed soon after the stump of the umbilical cord dries up and drops down. During the period of pollution the family does not take part in any ritual activities. Members of other families also do not accept food from this family. A fowl is given to the Oraon priest for sacrifice to protect the baby from evil spirits and evil eyes. On the day of purification the houses are cleaned and all clothes used by family members are washed. The traditional midwife and other women who conducted the delivery of the child, wash the clothes and mats used by the mother. The baby is bathed in tepid water. All male members of the family get their head hair cut. All persons who assisted at the time of delivery are entertained with festive meals and rice beer. The family invites friends and relatives if it can afford.

The name of the baby is selected from among the names of the dead ancestors through grain divination by an unmarried boy. On this occasion the head-hair of the baby is cut for the first time.

Marriage

The Oraons practise adult marriage. Pre-marital union and marriage within the own totemic group or with a person belonging to any other community are considered illegitimate. Preferential marriages like cross-cousin and levitate and sororate marriages are still in practice. Besides, marriage by elopement, marriage by capture and marriage by service are occasionally performed. But the most common but expensive type of marriage is held through negotiation. In this type of marriage, several visits are exchanged by both the parties to fix the amount of bride price and the date of marriage. The marriage takes place in girl's village. Smearing vermilion on each others forehead is the principal rite of the marriage. The occasion is celebrated with singing and dancing which continues for 3 to 4 days in both the villages. The guests and relatives are entertained with festive meals and rice beer.

Widow remarriage is socially approved. In most cases widows remarry widowers with the rare exception of those boys marrying their deceased elder brother's wife. Divorce by either side is permissible on grounds like adultery, laziness and bad temper with the approval of village Panchayat.

Death

The dead body with the exception of children and pregnant women is generally burnt. For those who die after the sprouting of the new paddy plants and before harvest, they practise provisional burial. In case of provisional burial, the remnants of the deceased are collected after harvest and then cremated. After cremation, all male members who attended the funeral, cut their head hair. Both men and women who attended the funeral, take bath and return to the house of the deceased for purifying themselves by the smoke emitting from the fire in grain husk and sprinkling water mixed with turmeric and oil on their heads. After this all present are entertained with rice beer. On the following day women go to collect the bones of the deceased. The bones of all cases of death in a village during the year are taken ceremonially for immersion in a river. The occasion is celebrated with dancing, singing and feasting.

Social Organisation and Social Control

The internal structure of the Oraon society is very elaborate. Risley H.H (1891) has mentioned that the tribe had five subtribes, viz. Bagra Oraon, Dhanka Oraon, Kharia Oraon, Khendro Oraon and Munda Oraon, who have in course of time, become strictly distinctive endogamous groups. The larger social groupings like phratry and moiety systems which are found among a few of the tribal groups of the state are absent among them.

At present the Oraon tribe is internally divided into a number of exogamous totemic clans known as *Gotra* or *Varga*. Each clan consists of a number of families which are distributed in different villages. S.C. Roy (1915) has given a long list of totemic clans of the Oraon of Chotanagpur. Both Dalton (1972) and Risley (1898) have furnished lists of clans found among them. Das and Raha (1963) have given a list of 38 totemic groups which they found among the Oraons of Sunderban in West Bengal. While mentioning the characteristics of the clan system among the Oraon, Roy (1915) writes, "totemism which was the basis of social and political organisation of the Oraons in what may be roughly called the hunting and pastoral stages of Oraon culture, still forms the fundamental feature of their social organization in so far as kinship, marriage and relations of the sexes are concerned. Among the Oraons of Orissa, only 17 totemic groups could be found. These are 1. *Tirki* (Mouse), 2. *Lakda*(Tiger), 3. *Linda* (a kind of eel), 4. *Kerketa* (Hedge sparrow), 5. *Gidhi* or *Gidhiar* (vulture), 6. *Toppo* (a species of long tailed bird fish), 7. *Ekka* (tortoise), 8. *Bakla* (a kind of grass), 9. *Bara* (Ficus Indica), 10. *Khes* (Paddy grain), 11. *Panna* (Iron), 12. *Bekh* (salt), 13. *Kujur* (a variety of wild fruit), 14. *Kispatta* (pig's entraits), 15. *Gari* (Monkey), 16. *Khakha* (raven). As regards the origin of these totems they have faint memory that the totemic plants, animals or objects are believed to have helped or protected the ancestors of the clan. Religious significance and observances of religious rites concerning the totems are not seen. Members of the totemic groups pay reverence to their respective totemic animals or plants whenever they come across. The taboo to use totemic objects which are indispensable in daily life is relaxed. For example, the members of *Bekh* (salt) clan do not eat raw salt but can take food in which salt is added. All members of a clan regard themselves as descendants of a common ancestor and as such marital relationship is strictly prohibited within the clan. Thus clans are exogamous and any sexual relationship among the members of the same clan is considered highly incestuous. If a person whether male or female breaks this rule he or she is ex-communicated which is irrevocable.

Oraons had a tradition of managing their own tribal affairs through multi-level panchayats. At the village level the *Mahato* (the secular headman) and the *Naega* (the Sacerdotal head) assisted by the *Pujari* or *Panbhara* and the village elders constitute the village panchayat to deal with offences and disputes such as theft, assault, division of property, divorce, offences relating to breach of clan rules and also sexual offences committed in the village. Beyond the village, a group of neighbouring villages of 10 to 12 constitute a Parha under the leadership of the *Mahato* of the important village. Here inter-village disputes are settled. But after their migration to Sundergarh area, the Oraon leadership was subjected to many factors which influenced and reduced the importance of their traditional leadership pattern. First of all the existing village administration under the leadership of the *Gauntia*, *Ganju*, *Parganadar*, etc gave the first blow to their traditional leadership. Secondly, the spread of Christianity and the statutory village panchayat reduced the importance of their traditional leadership. Their leadership pattern under the impact of caste Hindus has undergone several changes. Thus the traditional leadership based on age, experience, heritage is replaced by the new leadership based on occupation, wealth and political consciousness which is trying to bring reform in their society. However, their traditional priest till today continues to officiate in all ritual performances.

Religious Practices and the Belief System

Oraon religious beliefs and practices have been considerably influenced by Hinduism and Christianity. They believe in the existence of a number of Gods and Goddesses. Their supreme benevolent God is called *Dharani* who is equated with Sun God and is worshipped on every religious ceremony. According to their belief system the fate of the individual and the community depend on their relationship with the supernatural powers who intervene in human affairs by bringing diseases and hardship. They employ the village priest called *Naega* who belongs to their own group, whenever any misfortune befalls on an individual. Besides, the *Mati* is also consulted. They appease the supernatural powers by offering sacrifices through a series of rites and ceremonies round the year for their safety and protection. They observe religious rites connected with their economic pursuits and at each stage like birth, marriage and death of individuals. The important religious ceremonies such as *Phagu* in February-March to mark the end of the year and beginning of the new year, *Sarhul* in March-April before eating the new fruits and flowers of the forest, *Bisu-Sikar* (summer hunt) in April-May, *Jeth-Jatra* in May-June, *Jitua* in August-September and *Karma* in September-October. Besides all these they also observe *Kalipuja* and *Dashera* along with their Hindu neighbours. Those who have been converted to Christianity observe the festivals of their new faith. All these occasions including the ceremonies observed in connection with birth, marriage and death are celebrated with appropriate communal dancing and singing.

Economic Life

The Oraons are described as an agricultural community. Though it is true that the major segment of the Oraon population by possessing some acreage of agricultural land adhere to agriculture, there has been considerable diversification in their occupational pattern. The dependence on agricultural labour is less among the Oraons while employment in mining and quarrying and in manufacturing, processing, servicing and repairing under industrial sector has shown a rising trend. They have also an appreciable quota of workers in household industry.

The crops grown are mainly used for their own consumption. Their principal crop is rice which is generally grown once in a year and occasionally twice by a limited number of households which have irrigation facilities. They also grow millets, pulses and vegetables during Kharif and Rabi seasons. They sell the surplus agricultural produce for cash with which they buy clothes and other necessities of life. Cultivation is primarily a family function. Sometimes a household seeks the help and cooperation of close relatives on reciprocal basis. The households having larger holdings engage either labourers on daily payment basis or keep attached labourers preferably of their own group to assist them in different agricultural operations.

Besides cultivation, some of them have earned proficiency in rural crafts such as carpentry, tile and brick moulding and rope making. Women still weave mat from date-palm leaf and make broom sticks from wild grass. Persons working in mining and quarries and in industrial establishments both as skilled and unskilled workers constitute a sizeable section in the workers' community. Hunting, fishing and collection of forest produce have been given up due to the absence of forest.

The weekly market plays an important role both in their economic and social life. This not only provides opportunity to sell surplus agricultural produce and to purchase daily necessities of life, but also to meet the kinsmen living in distance places.

In Orissa, the Oraon are one of the most progressive tribes. In the field of agriculture they use chemical fertilizers, pesticides, improved seeds and modern techniques and do not suffer from indebtedness. They have also availed themselves of the opportunities to improve their economic conditions through various special programmes like ITDA, ERRP and IRDP. They are labourious and therefore some of the family members migrate to other places for wage earning during the period when there is no work at home.

Majority of them earn adequately to maintain themselves and to purchase varieties of modern articles like watch, radio, cycle, motor cycle, dresses and other household articles. Now they save money to built assets for themselves.

FOLKLORE OF ORAONS

Like the Santals and Kharias, the Oraons also have developed a culture of their own which is reflected in their myths, legends and folklores. These myths, legends and folklores have been transcended in verbal language from generation to generation.

For the people of the Oraon villages, songs and dances appear to absorb their time particularly at night. In summer and winter nights both young boys and girls are seen dancing and singing at the village *akhara* from evening till midnight and even much later. And on occasions of their religious festivals they also spend the whole day in singing and dancing.

In the following paragraphs we have tried to present some collections of Oraon myths, legends and folklores.

MYTHS

Myths of Origin

1. Once a saint was meditating in a cave near a waterfall in a hill. While he was engrossed in his meditation, ants climbed over him and made an ant-hill. A woodcutter cut it thinking it a trunk of a tree. Blood started flowing from the saint's waist which he collected in an utensil. A boy and a girl (brother and sister) were born out of that blood. The offsprings of these two came to be known as Kudukh community. The people of this Kudukh community were called savage people or primitive community and according to the Kudukh language they were called *Singristia*. Then again the children of these communities were called Urujan (Born from plant). Gradually this word became extinct and was pronounced as Oraon.

2. During the reign of Ram the monkeys were the ancestors of the Oraon community. When Ram went to northern India and died, the people of this community mourned over his death saying 'oh Ram', 'oh Ram'. Gradually with the passage of time 'oh Ram' became Oraon.

3. It is a populated community and the people are known as the sons of *Ravana*, as *Ravana* had one lakh sons and sixteen lakhs grandsons. This word was first recognised as 'Raon' and later with the change of alphabet came to be known as Oraon and then gradually became 'Uram'.

Myth Regarding Name, Clan and Establishment of the Kingdom

Oraons had village panchayat. But no king was ruling over it. The kingdom was established in the following way according to the opinion of the people.

During the burning of the Khandab forest by Lord Krishna and Arjuna at the time of Mahabharat, the people of the snake community went to another place and from amongst them a Cobra named Vasuki went to Varanaṣi. There he lived in the guise of a Brahmin and married a Brahmin girl Parvati. They came to a place called

Swetambe close to Chotanagpur, later the wife realised that her husband was a snake. After coming to know this Vasuki left Parvati and drowned himself in a nearby pond when the birth of his son took place near that pond. The child was covered by the hood of a snake which was noticed by a Brahmin. The Brahmin took the child to the nearby village Swetambe and left the child with a Oraon family. When he grew up the chiefs of Oraon community elected him as their king.

Spiritual Ideology of Kudukh

Kirodandi is the religion of the *Kudukh* community. According to this religion Lord Khasuanladha in the guise of a deformed man directed others to have worldly desires which contributed to the development of a religion of the forefathers of the *Kudukh* community.

According to this religion they make a diagram of a square colouring it with black, white and red. Then they put some white rice in the middle of the square and an egg on top of it. They put a broken stick on the egg. They put that rice in a fan made of bamboo and sit in front of the diagram. Thereafter they perform Yagyan by reciting the whole spiritual principles in the form of song. Here they do not worship any

god. They consider god as formless, all powerful, almighty and supreme.

Beside *Kirodandi*, the *Kudukh* community also muses over the soul of their forefathers. They call the soul of their forefathers '*Panchbala*'. They believe that if they will muse *Panchbala* it will save them from all dangers. Thus while eating their food they offer a little amount on the floor in respect of their God. They offer different delicacies to their deities on different festivals. This process is called '*Sitiasma*'. On every festival they throw three drops of wine at the two corners of the door before drinking it.

LEGENDS

Tattoo mark

The story originates from the time since the Muslims were ruling our country. At that time the Oraons were living as per their customs and traditions. Many a time the male members used to go to forest for hunting, carrying their bows and arrows. As hunting was also one of their traditions, during this period they used to hunt many wild animals, such as wild boar, deer and hare etc. This took two to three days taking benefit of which the Muslims misbehaved with the female members of that society. When this became unbearable the Oraons fought with the Muslims and defeated them thrice, but finally the Oraons were defeated. Therefore, the female members put three black marks on the head of each member of the tribe as a sign of bravery. From that day onwards all the Oraons have three black marks on their head.

Kisan and Oraon

Once upon a time there lived an Adivasi community in a place near present day Chotanagpur. Once the Dravidas attacked them for which they were separated into two groups. Near Chotanagpur there is a hill named *Pithagola*. Kisans and Oraons have set up their settlements on both sides of this hill. When the Dravidas attacked them, in retaliation these Adivasis threw mudballs at them which piled up in the size of that hill. And that hill separated the Adivasies into two groups. The Adivasis who took up farming were recognized as Kisan and others became Oraon. However there is a dispute regarding their seniority. Some say that the Kisans are elder brothers whereas the others say the Oraons are the elder brothers.

Karama tree

On the occasion of *Sarhul* the male members went for hunting. Taking advantage of it the Muslims attacked the females of the tribe. In retaliation the Oraon females under the leadership of Princess Singhi wore male attires, picked up swords and fought against the enemies. They defeated the enemies thrice. But the enemies attacked them stealthily in the night and defeated them. As a result the Oraons went into the jungle and hid inside a big cave. They even came near the cave, but could not find the Adivasis as a big *karama* tree which was there in front of the cave had kept the cave hidden. As a result the enemies could not find the Adivasis and thus they were saved. Therefore all Adivasis (Oraons) have been paying respect to the *karama* tree.

STORIES

Dharama and Karama

Once upon a time there lived two brothers Dharama and Karama by name. Dharma was the elder one and Karama was the younger one. The elder brother always remained engrossed in religious discussions. He had one pre-conceived notion that it is impossible to live in this world without religion. As he was a godfearing person, he used to dress differently. Gradually, he became a young man, after which he renounced his home and went to the forest. There he built one hermitage surrounded by trees and through meditation became a sage. On the other hand Karama was a hard working boy. He had a belief that if he worked hard he would find god. From his limited landed property he was earning and living happily along with his wife and child. Karama always used to think, 'if my elder brother had been there he would have helped me in farming, but now there is nobody to help me'. Thinking in such a manner he decided to search for his brother and bring him home. Therefore he carried some food with him and left his house in search of his brother. Roaming around in the forest he became tired and at the fall of dusk he looked for a place to sleep. Finally, he found a cave and stayed there overnight. Next morning he again searched for his brother and finally found him meditating in his hermitage. After the meditation was over, Karama requested him to return home. But his elder brother refused. Ultimately Karama returned home with great disappointment.

Cow and her Master

There was a healthy, milch cow, who had already given birth to two to three calves. Once one of the legs of the cow was broken for which she could not go for grazing. As a result the cow gradually became weak and stopped giving milk. Therefore, her owner started disliking the cow and always thought it would be better if the cow would die. Once a friend had come to his house who saw the cow in pain and suggested the owner to kill her and sell the meat. The owner agreed to his suggestions and together they planned and took the cow to a hill and killed her there by hitting her with a stone. They sold the meat to the Christians staying nearby at a very cheap rate who celebrated by having feast with the meat received at such a cheap rate.

From the next day onwards the cow was not found. When the neighbours asked the owner regarding the cow, he fumbled for which the neighbours suspected him. Gradually, the truth came out and in the village a meeting was called to punish the culprit. '*Pahan*', the political head of the village presided over the meeting and after trial, the culprit was declared accused and as compensation he gave a feast to his society where he promised that he would never again kill a cow. But simultaneously it was also decided in the meeting that there was no harm in eating the meat of a dead cow.

Koel and Sankh

Once upon a time in a Oraon family there lived two sisters, at their maternal uncle's house. The maternal uncle used to love them immensely. But the maternal aunt had just the reverse attitude towards them. Once she sent both the sisters to work in the field. While working a storm came suddenly and therefore both the sisters got drenched in the pouring water of the storm, but continued their work. After it rained their uncle went to the field in search of the two girls. But to his great disappointment and dismay he could not find them. While returning back, both the sisters appeared before him in the form of two snakes and said, 'we can never be converted again into human beings, therefore from now onwards we will flow as two rivers'. All our community people will live on our banks. The name of those two sisters were 'Sankh' and 'Koel'. Accordingly both the rivers were also named as Sankh and Koel which began to flow separately in search of each other and finally met at a point (Vedavyas). At Vedvyasa a temple was built where they are being worshipped till today.

SONGS

The Oraons have songs appropriate to their different dances. The songs are distinguished from one another in rhythm and the manner of singing. All Oraon songs are primarily meant to be sung in accompaniment of dances and the names of songs are in accordance with the different kinds of dances.

Yatra Songs

1. *Radhe Kalachiya Bhaiya Naena*
   Singar Relan Kala Chiya
   Radhe Ranchi Lahar Daga
   Bichiya Khedange Kalachiya Bhaili
   Naena Singar Pelan Kalchiya

Meaning :

The girl's brother is talking to his parents that our daughter is expert in dance and music, so we will not deny her for her jewelleries. We will bring for her ornaments from Ranchi and Lahardaga.

2. *Paienya Manja Jiage Jhajhat*
   Ayang Bangaru Nao Dechar
   Bharsi Natir Patari Bidiar
   Nalaghi Saman Yang Bangaru

Meaning

It is very cold during winter. Oraons are very poor. So in regret they are saying - burning all the paddy and placing a cot near it, we will sleep like a dog and spend the whole winter.

3. *Runu Runu Runu Nalkha*
Chaokhe Nisan Bataginu, Radhe
Batagi Runu Runu
Runu Nalakha Chakhen Kan Bataginu Badhe

Meaning

Runu is the name of a sag (green vegetable). He sowed that sag and ploughed the field with the bullocks and sowed the Runu sag.

4. *Radhe Salu Shuga Ame Anakai*
Ade Lanke Gala Radhe
Aienti Paienti Narika Nasan
Ninjar Ambhe Salu Suga
Ame Anakar
Radhe Relagadi Nekashe Sundar
Gucha Nerakao, Radhe Kiyanu
Panna Pakhna, Meyanu Chityanu
Banga Lagi

Meaning

How beautiful is the train, come let us go to see it. Iron and stones are spread down, the train is looking very beautiful while moving on the iron bars and stones which are spread on earth.

Karama

1.
Garagaran Malu Makhan Cheon
Papan Makhan Nay Checn Papan
Makhan
Mannenu Chundiyan, Keteranu
Tiliyan
Daudanu Nuyan Tawanu Kirindi
Ant Duunnu
Sajwan Tantar Nu Nathran
Daudanu
Nuyan, Bijay Papa Nida Nanta
Kida, Mala Biti Papa

Meaning

Oh mother do not eat bitter peels and chappati (the cake made of chenpapa oil). The mother is telling her daughter, "this year there is famine, so there will be no cake". Still as the daughter is not responding, she explained how she managed to make the cake.

By the wooden part of the iron pipe, the rice was powdered, strained it with the bamboo strainer, then kept it in the basket. By keeping the pan on the mud burner, mixed the sugarcandy with water and boiled this water which is kept in a bowl (Mixing of sugarcandy with water is called *lindiyan*).

2. *Karama Ta Chali Gelaen*
Nahiyar Desare, Karama Ta Chali Gelaen
Nahiyar Desare, Nakhera Chelaen
Karama Galaen, Kon Bhaiya
Upsana Kone Bheja Piyas
Chalaja Karama Ko Sebayege
Chete Bhaiya Upasana Bale
Bhaya Piyasa, Chota Bhaiya
Upasa Bale, Bhaiya Piyasa
Chalacha Karama Ka Seba

Meaning

Karama branch is gone to clean the space, making a gathering there. They planted the karama branch there. Younger brother remained in fasting, elder brother remained without eating and drinking while looking after the karama.

Dhulia Karama

1. *Hare, Ninganege Pello*
Thonte Poko Chaba, Nighanpello
Nechehoda Bao - 2
Nighae Jodi Jonkhas Koda
Raji Keras. Nighan Pello
Ne Chchada Bao................Sona.

Meaning

You, daughter Thanto: Ants will bite you. Who will leave you, your friend has gone abroad. Who will leave you, who will console you.

2. *Koili Par Jonkhar Pahinana*
Barechar, Hare Jea, Bujhura
Lagi .... Sona Nadi ....
Bhogan Dara Baron Yayo
Banga Ghatino Chekron Yao Dengo

Meaning

My heart is not accepting the guests coming from the other side of Koel river. Don't get me married father and mother. Rivers and canals are full and are glittering. If you will get me married, how I will comeback, I will not be able to cross the rivers, the boat will stick to the bank of the river.

Asali Karama

1. *Konkolokoe Pelle Rapanida*
Kera
Bakla Lekha Laya Koya Mani
Bhai
Bakla ....
Bakila Kalobhe Ramanida
Kere ....
Bakila Lekhe Laya Kayamani
Bhai

Meaning

Tall, slim female is sowing the paddy. While sowing, she is bending this side and that side like a crane. For the sake of the crane she went to sow the paddy, bending here and there like a crane.

2. *Guchcha Bhaiya Sendera Tonka*
Thana Harina Chocha Bhaiya Tana ....
Tana Hauva Chocha Bhaiya Ghatinu Chekchar
Bhaiya Ghati Cheka Chae.
Ghati Chekechae Yao.
Hissa Pata Lagiya Bhaiya - 2
Hissapata Lagiya Bhaiya.
Hisapata Lagiya
Hisapata Lagiya Yayo
Khojdim Game Gacha Sona-2
Khojdim Game Kacha Yaye
Sone Giridhan Nitiya Ayo
Chape Giridhin Nitia

Meaning

Come brother, let's go for hunting. The deer stopped from the right side.

After returning from hunting the mother asked her son and her son is replied "On the way we killed a bison. After killing it, we dissected it and kept it in a small basket. In this process the smell spread in the village, by smelling it, the hawks came down to earth".(This is the conversation between the mother and son).

Karama Lujhuri

1. *Ghaghari Partanu Khel Saman Kharkhi.... 2*
Hay Hay Ghuchnay Nelakata Jankhae Pellaerin
Kalega Khot Nayen Negane Barat ....
Hae Hae Daherenta Gol Pandrin Dhara Dhara Haat....

Meaning :

The conversation is between mother and daughter. Daughter, O daughter "the drum is being beaten at the Ghaghari mountain. Come lets go to see the dancing boys and girls".

Mother

We will go, but with whom will we return.
On the way will take along the untouchables
and lower castes.

Sarhul

1. *Kaddi -*
Kalako Kala Nuyange
Tikarinu Namba Sekera
Kalako Kala Nuyange Pisa
Manje Dhara Chandwan Khel Khelo Khelo
Pairi Biri Nuyan Kalako Nadt.
Biri Kal Khasane
Kala Ko Kala Nuiyan Gage
Pisa Manje Dhara Chandwan
Khel Khel O Khel

Meaning

Go out soon to plough and don't sit under the sun. Later you will wash your necklace (the necklace made of silver coin). In the morning go for ploughing. In the afternoon go to make ridge in the field, in the evening you will wash your silver necklace.

Sarhul (Oraon song, p. 274, 'The Oraons of Chotanagpur')

2. *Jambu dahuran laoa, dada !*
Binrio kamon;
Ningusan bheja bechon.
Jambu dahuran laoa, dada !
Binrio kamon.

Meaning

In this song a child tells her friend to bring a blackberry twig for her with which she wants to make ear-sticks. She also wants to dance with her friend.

Jadur (Oraon song, p. 273, 'The Oraons of Chotanagpur')

1. *Guch, pelo, kalot koe, Tiko dhorha,*
Guch, pelo, kalot koe, namhae patra
Namhae patra, pelo, atkha chokhot,
Tiko dhora, pelo, injo pithot.

Meaning

This song is about Oraon girls. A girl calls her friends to go to the village forest and gather leaves. She also wants all of them then to go to the *'Tiko'* stream for catching fish.

Kharia (Oraon song, p. 274, 'The Oraons of Chotanagpur')

1. *Sira-Sita-nalnu, kakro-lata-erpa-nu,*
Bhaia-bahin rachar, Sira-Sita-nalnu.
Chiro barung kundia.
Juri-juri rahachkat, bhaiare !
Panti-panti rahachkat, bhaiare !
Kakro-lata-erpa, bhaiare !
Sea-lata radat, bhaiare !
Dharti-nu radat, bhaiare !

Meaning

The song narrates the life of a brother and sister who live in a carb-hole in a field called *Sira-Sita* where a kind of grass called *chiro-grass* is growing. This is what a girl narrates to her brother.

Jhumar (Oraon song, p. 276, 'The Oraons of Chotanagpur')

1. *Eka-pelo-gahi samae kera ?*
Eka-pelo-gahi samae kera ?
Ganga-Jamunanu birio bohail goe, sajan !
Chenra pelo-gahi samae kera !
Chenra pelo-gahi samae kera !
Ganga Jamunanu birio bohail goe, sajan !

Meaning

This is a sad song which describes the death of a little girl. It says that she came to the world for a very short time and that time has already passed. It expresses sorrow and shock over her death.

Karam (Oraon song, p. 276, 'The Oraons of Chotanagpur')

3. *Urbarghi tangda banna kichri, koe,*
Pachri hedde ijki rai !
Randi pachcho tangeda ledera kichiri,
Rajham-rajhamra bheja bichi !

Meaning

In this song a comparison is made between rich and poor. It says that the daughter of a rich man has worn colourful dress but stood joylessly at a distance. But on the other hand the daughter of a widow who is poorly dressed is jumping and dancing merrily with her friends.

DANCE

Ordinarily it is after their evening meals that the young men assemble at the *Akhara* and begin to dance and sing. This is the signal given to the girls to come out of their houses and join the dance. In less than half an hour's time we could see the young men and women all at their respective places on the dancing ground. The most important events in the life of an Oraon are love and marriage. In different seasons different events take place in accompaniment of dances and songs. The year begins after the harvesting of low land paddy in November-December. The period from the harvesting till March is the merriest season of the year. This is the season when the granary is full and there is much less work to do and this is the time when the Oraon young boys and girls fall in love with each other caluminating in marriage. This is also the season when they celebrate different festivals. They observe the wedding and courtship of their deceased relatives.

The festival which is observed on this occasion is called '*Har-gouri Jatra*'. It is only after this occasion that marriages are celebrated among those who have survived. The dances which are performed on the occasion of marriage are called '*Jadur*' dances. Thus the Oraons observe different festivals in different seasons and their dances are of different types.

The Mundas

THE MUNDA TRIBES

The Munda in their physical features belong to the North Munda group to which the Santal, the Ho, The Kolha belong. With a keen sense of self-respect and an eye for love and things of beauty, truthful, hardworking and honest, suspicious of aliens and with a craze for *handia* (rice beer). The Mundas are akin to those belonging to the North Munda racial stock. They are noted for their dance and music, their songs depicting beauty of nature and sincerity and depth of love for their lovers and their life partners. Their songs composed by these graphically the inner sentiments and emotions and portray their joy and love and their sorrows and limitations which their surroundings create for them.

Of all the impulses that inspire the Munda poets the feelings for love are perhaps the strongest. The passion of human heart which envelopes the poetical activity of the Munda mind is reflected in the voluntary and spontaneous outcome of the songs depicting joys and sorrows of their life partners and companions in all walks of their life. Out of a huge stock of Munda love songs only a few of them are reproduced below from the writings of Sarat Chandra Roy. The songs which are mentioned below are reproduced from his book. The Mundas and their country.

LAHSUA (Munda song P. 327 'The Mundas and their Country')

1. *Bo tama risa risa*
Supid kedam ranga nacha,
Nida singi, ba-gem gututana.
Nama nagen jige lotana !
Andutadam sakomtadam,
Hotore do hisir mena,
Polatamdo Chilka saritana,
Nama nagen jige lotana.

Meaning

This song expresses the romantic feeling of a man for his beloved. It gives a vivid description of the woman's adornment. The woman looks so beautiful in her adornment that inspires a man to sing a song of this type.

LAHSUA (Munda song P. 327 'The Mundas and their Country')

2. *Alom maire kakapajia*
Nama nagen lotana hia,
Namo dinda naio dinda,
Da chatu jeson binda,
Alom maire kakapajia,
Nama nagen lotana hia.

Meaning

This song is an expression of love of a young man for his beloved. In the song, he requests the young woman not to be cruel to him and he offers his love-filled heart to her. The young man compares his match with the young woman to that of a pitcher on its straw-made stand.

LAHSUA (Munda song P. 328 'The Mundas and their Country')

3. *Bhati orea piti piri, honortanaking juri juri,*
Niral sobha nelotanaking, kulgeaking bano hiating.
Nawa hiriti piritiking, bani hiating, re-gating.
Samrom rupa munga mala, sasang-sari katare pola
Jiure do rajijanaking, bano hiating, re gating.
Nawa hiriti piritiking, bano hiating, re gating

Meaning

This song describes about love between a young man

and a young woman. The poet is filled with joy when he sees the enchanting sight of a couple roaming around hand-in-hand in their beautiful attire. The care-free attitude and fearless behaviour of the lovers have deeply impressed the poet.

JAPI (Munda song P. 337 'The Mundas and their Country')

1. *Chetan kutire, gosain,*
Terea tereako, gosain
Latar kutire gosain,
Marea, mareako,
Sari, japi sari
Rutaba saili do, gosain,
Rukuken rukuken, gosain,
Saidaba sukuri, gosain,
Chotabaken, chotabaken
Sari japi sari
Tuiu mendo gore, gosain
Rukuken rukuken, gosain.
Terangi mendo, gosain,
Chotabaken chotabaken,
Sari japi sari
Torahoe togejan, gosain
Chutima kanasul, gosain
Torahoe togejan, gosain
Subama serom gosain.
Sari japi sari
Torahoe senojan, gosain
Singeko birite gosain,
Sair japi sari.
Torahoe senojan gosain
Madeko landirite, gosain,
Sari japi sari

Meaning

In this song, a description is given about a hunt of the Mundas. The poet describes his joy over seeing the movement of games in fear when the hunters passionately follow them. The poet also gives a picturesque account of the natural surrounding.

JADUR (Munda song P. 352 'The Mundas and their Country')

1. *Kolikata telengako rakablena,*
Nokore najinako derakeda ?
Sarghati sahebko uparlena,
Chimaere najinako basakeda ?
Mena menado Ranchipiri,
Ranchi pirire derakeda.
Mena menado Durundabadi,
Durunda badireko baasa-keda,
Ranchi-pirireko dera-keda,
Ranchi-piri kare nekelajana.
Durunda-badireko baasa-keda,
Durunda-badi chiru taiurtana.

Meaning

This song is a eulogy of some soldiers who came from Calcutta to Ranchi as saviour of the Mundas. In this song, an inquisitiveness is shown to know from the grandmother as to what happened when the soldiers or British Sahebs came and camped in that place.

CONCLUSION

An Account of unwritten literary world of tribal communities

The unwritten literary world of the tribal community comprises very rich Oral Literature or Folklore. The word folklore was first employed in a letter signed by Ambrose Merton published in the Athenaeum of London, 22 August, 1946. Its writer urged that accounts of the manners, customs, observances, superstitions, ballads, proverbs etc. of the olden time be recorded so that later students could turn for information to these dying remnants of the unrecorded past which were termed popular Antiquities or Oral Literature. In a broader sense the folklore generally comprises the least tangible expression of the aesthetic aspects of culture. In other words, it consists of myths, tales, proverbs, riddles, metaphors and verses and folk speech. Dance and music of the tribal communities are also part of the folkore. To a varying degree these components combine with each other and with the graphic and plastic arts. They make up the rituals and other forms of group expression including dance and folk drama.

Various authorities have defined folklore in various ways. One of the traditional meanings of the folklore is Oral Tradition. William Bascoms has defined in a narrow sense which includes folk-tales, myths, legends, folk songs, ballads, epics and poems, proverbs and riddles. Folklore is defined by Encyclopedia Britannica as a folk learnings and all knowledge that is transmitted by word of mouth and all crafts and techniques that are learned by imitation as well as the products of these arts. Some authors like Taylor have included the language in the folklore.

Taking all these definitions into consideration the folklore can be described under four major items. They are

1. Folk literature
2. Folk art (including dance),
3. Folk belief and custom and
4. Folk crafts and languages

Folklore performs various functions. Myths explain the universe and provide a basis for ritual performances and religious belief systems. Folk-tales instead are of secular character. The folk-tales are regarded as unwritten records of tribal history. These tales serve to maintain a sense of group identity and unity. Proverbs including riddles speak of experiences which are gained by observing events of day to day life. The riddles particularly serve as a test of wits. Anatole France has given some idea about the role which folklore plays. According to him the folklore is looked upon as mythology on which Nations thrive. He said that from legends the nonliterate communities draw all the ideas necessary for their existence.

The stories are told chiefly for recreation, but in many areas they are taken as myth to explain some of the important phenomena of the universe. Animal stories are widely spread. These stories narrate the wit of some animals and foolishness of other animals. Folk tales as they travel from one place to other change in their contents and purpose. Some time the tales lose their sacred character and become secular in nature.

The stories are composed of three elements such as character, incident and plot. These elements are independently variable and can move in groupings and in any combinations. In certain cases different characters will be found performing the sequence of acts which constitute the incidence which in turn makes up a specific plot. A given character may move from tale to tale and serves different motifs. Motifs combine themselves into many plots and that is why the analysis of such variants is an important function of the folklorists.

Folk-tales are great travelers. It is very important and fascinating to show how the tales have changed in their travel to fit into different natural settings and different cultural matrix.

A folk-tale incorporates details of an earlier period in the history of a people who tell it. The folk-tale documents their earlier life.

The folklore reflects the life of a people and reveals their aspirations, values and goals. Different people enjoy different ranks in society. The folklore particularly the myths reveal the rank of a people in society. Proverbs are generally used to express something in an indirect fashion. Many people don't like to rebuke a person or use certain words which carries insult to him. In such cases proverbs are used expressing indirectly what a person has in mind by way of rebuking or insulting a person.

Folklore expresses hidden reactions of people to social sanctions. In this case a psychoanalytic machanism is at work wherein customary behaviour is distorted in a manner that indicates the desires which the individuals must supress so as to confirm to the ways of their society. Folklore creates a world where vindications are granted. There are stories which reveal the weak prevailing over the strong or where the evil meets an avenger. The folklore particularly certain stories create conditions where unpleasant conditions in life are resolved in ways which are not those of the work a day world.

By folklore it means that the myth, lore, riddle and proverbs which the folklore comprises are thought to be a monopoly of unliterate or tribal people. Societies whether they are literate or not have their lore. But the popular stories and sayings are generally not reduced to writing among the literate people. It is only the Anthropologists or folklorists who take up studies of literate societies and do not generally miss this aspect of folklore in their ethnographic studies.

The study of folklore as a cultural phenomenon aids significantly in the understanding of the culture of which it is a part. The study of tales may be cited to illustrate the point. Each tale in itself is cluster of elements which are independently variable and the study of a tale yields materials for the understanding of how any complex of cultural traits can vary in transmission from one community to the other.

The folktales are stable and tenacious and this factor helps in reconstructing the contacts of the communities with one another and in understanding the diffusion of cultural traits.

The study of tales in different communities reveals variations in typology of the tales. Among certain communities the tales are more or less of explanatory type and among other communities the tales are of trickster type and still in certain other communities the tales show preoccupation with celestial phenomena. If one tribe speaks of tales of the type of creation myths another tribe narrates myths about cataclysms. Similarly other tribal communities have oral literatures which are full of myths relating to transformation of men into animals and vice versa, star myths, tales explaining the origin of world, institutions and rites and rituals and stories about animals, ghosts, spirits and deities.

Lastly it can be said that the study of folklore throws light on literacy qualities of the tales, myths, legends, riddles, proverbs, ballads and all those which the folklore contains. It is necessary to collect large number of tales and myths from a single society and study these scientifically using proper methods of analysis so that the ways by which plots of the stories are developed and the mechanisms that are developed to sustain interest in them and achieve adequate characteristics, can be found for cross-cultural comparative analysis.

GLOSSARY

Abge Bonga	:	Bonga living in house
Ahiri Pipiri	:	Two mythical persons
Akhara	:	Assembly
Baha	:	First fruit of Mohua offered to Jaher deities
Baha Bonga	:	Flower Festival (Santal)
Bakla	:	A kind of grass
Balakala Serenj	:	A type of marriage song
Bandra	:	Monkey
Bansa	:	Lineage
Peterbale	:	Banyan tree
Bapla	:	Marriage
Baram	:	Jungle spirit
Bariyat	:	People
Barla	:	Ficus indica
Basumata	:	Mother earth
Bekh	:	Salt
Bhitar	:	Sacred place in the house
Bisu-Sika	:	Summer hunt
Bonga	:	Deity
Buru Bonga	:	Hill deities
Chaichampa	:	A place name
Changu dance	:	Dance in accompaniment of changu musical instruments
Dahar Serenj	:	Ritual songs about natural phenomena

Damodar Jatra	:	Immersion of bones
Dang Serenj	:	Marriage song sung by both bride and bridegroom sides
Dehuri	:	Kharia village priest
Dhangar	:	Unmarried Oraon in local Hindi
Dharam	:	Supreme deity
Dharani	:	Oraon supreme deity
Diku	:	Marriage by negotiation
Dipil	:	Marriage type
Dong	:	Marriage songs
Duar Itutee	:	Marriage type
Durang	:	Marriage song
Erok-sim	:	Sowing seeds
Ganag	:	Bride price
Ghat	:	A place in the bank of a river where people take bath
Gidhi or Gidhiar	:	Vulture
Golang	:	Rice beer
Gotra	:	Clan
Guldavnapam	:	A type of marriage
Gurakhu	:	Tobacco paste
Handia	:	Rice beer
Hansda	:	Duck
Harihara-sim	:	Offering of first millet crop
Hons and Hanseli	:	Two birds
Jahera	:	Ritual place of the Santals
Jaher aaya	:	Supreme goddess of Santals
Janthar	:	Winter rice crop
Jog Manjhi	:	Moral guardian of the village youth
Jonkh	:	Unmarried Oraon
Kachhu	:	Tortoise
Karam Siram	:	A tree
Karea	:	The cloth of the male child
Kardhani	:	The dress of the young Oraon
Kareya	:	The cloth of the Oraon male
Kendu tree	:	Rotten Diaspyres Melanoxylon

Keranga cloth	:	Cloth woven by strands made from the bark of Keranga tree)
Kerketa	:	Hedge sparrow
Khade-matkam	:	Mahula or Mahua tree
Khakha	:	Raven
Khandanugulli	:	A type of saree given to mother at the time of her daughter's marriage
Khanria	:	Piece of cloth which the Oraon women wear.
Khes	:	Paddy grain
Kispatta	:	Pig's entraits
Kudum	:	The merry making part on the occasion of marriage.
Kujur	:	A variety of wild fruit
Kutumba	:	Lineage group
Ladka	:	Tiger
Lagene	:	Dance on the occasion of birth
Lapez tiril	:	Kendu tree
Mag Bonga	:	First festival of a year celebrated in February
Magha-sim	:	End of the year
Manjhi	:	Secular headman
Manjhi Haram Bonga	:	Bonga of village headman
Manjhi-than	:	Ritual spot
Manmis	:	Babies
Marandi	:	Weed
Mukhi	:	Mid-wife
Murmu	:	Cow
Naega	:	Oraon village priest
Naik	:	Village priest
Naria tiles	:	Khappar
Ojha	:	The medicine man cum spirit doctor
Panchbala	:	Soul of the forefathers
Panna	:	Iron
Paramanik	:	Assistant headman
Paris	:	The division of the tribe into clans

Putli	:	The cloth of the female child
Saharas	:	The tree
Sari Sarjam	:	Sal tree
Sange	:	More
Sange Bariyat	:	Marriage type
Serenj	:	Song
Sindur	:	Marriage type
Sing Bonga	:	Supreme deity
Singrisita	:	People of the Kuduku community
Thakur	:	Supreme deity
Tirki	:	Mouse
Toppo	:	A species of fish
Tunki	:	A type of marriage

◆◆◆

BIBLIOGRAPHY

Archer, W.G. : *Mara Hapram Reak Katha (in Santali) (Santal pargana: Banerjee Press, 1969).*

— : *Hill of Flutes: Love and Poetry in Tribal India: A Portrait of the Santals (London: George Allen and Unwin, 1974).*

Archer, W.G. : *Tribal Law and Justice (A Report on the Santal) (New Delhi : Concept Publishing Company, 1984).*

Bag, Dhanapati : *In the Midst of Santals (Calcutta: Subarnarekha, 1987).*

Bhattacharya, P.N. : *'A Genetical Study of the Santals of Santal Parganas', The Anthropologist, Special Volume, 93, 1969, p. 104.*

Bhavani, Enakshi : *Folk and Tribal Designs of India (Bombay: D.B. Taraporevala Sons and Company, 1974).*

Biswas, P.C. : *The Santals of Santal Parganas (New Delhi: Bharatiya Adimjati Sevak Sangh, 1956).*

Bodding, P.O. : *Traditions and Institutions of the Santals (Oslo: A.W.Brog. Boktry., 1942).*

Bodding, P.O. : *Santal Folk Tales (Vo. I,II & III) (New Delhi : Gyan Publishing House, 1990)*

Bodding, P.O. : *A Chapter of Santal Folklore (Kristiania : A.W. Broggers Boktrykkeri A.S., 1924).*

Bodding, P.O. : *Studies in Santal Medicine and Connected Folklore (Calcutta : The Asiatic Society, 1925-40).*

Bompas, Cecil Henry : *Folklore of the Santal Parganas (New Delhi : Ajay Book Service, 1981).*

Campbcll, A. : *Santal Folk-Tales (Pokhuria: Santal Mission Press, 1891).*

Choudhury, S. et al : *'Study of Blood Groups and Haemoglobin Variants Among the Santal Tribe in Midinapur District of West Bengal', American Journal of Physical Anthropology, 26, 1967, pp. 307-12.*

Culshaw, W.J. : *Tribal Heritage: A Study of the Santals (London: Butterworth Press, 1949).*

Das, Gupta and Narendra Kumar : *Problems of Tribal Education and the Santals (New Delhi: Bharatiya Adimjati Sevak Sangh, 1963).*

Das, K.B. and L.K. Mahapatra : *Folklore of Orissa (New Delhi : National Book Trust, 1979, rpt. 1993)*

Dutta Majumdar, N. : *The Santal: A Study in Culture Change (Calcutta: Anthropological Survey of India, 1956).*

Duyker, Edward. : *Tribal Guerillas: The Santals of West Bengal and the Naxalite Movement (Delhi: Oxford University Press, 1987).*

Gausdal, J. : *The Santal Khuts: Contributions to Animistic Research (Oslo: Institute Sammenling Kulturforsk, 1960).*

Gautam, M.K. : *In Search of an Identity: A Case of the Santal of Northern India (Leiden: E.J. Brill, 1978).*

George, Somen E. : *The Dynamics of Santal Traditions in a Peasant Society (New Delhi: D.K. Publishers, 1979).*

Gini, Ashok : *'Some Genetic Markers in Tribals of Eastern India', Acta Anthropogenetica, 6 (2), 1982, pp. 99-106.*

Kochar, V.K. : *'Village Deities of the Santal and Associated Rituals', Anthropos, 61, 1966, pp. 241-57.*

KacAlpin, M.C. : *Report on the Condition of Santhals in the Districts of Birbhum, Bankura, Midnapore and North*

Balasore (Calcutta: Bengal Secretariat Press, 1909, rpt. 1981, Calcutta: Firma Mukhopadhyay).

Macphail, J.J. : *Three Months in Camp: Being the Daily Journal of a Medical Missionary on Tour Among the Santals (Pokhuria: Manbhum, Santal Mission Press, 1893).*

Mahapatra, S. : *Modernization and Ritual: Identity and Change in Santal Society (Calcutta: Oxford University Press, 1986).*

Mahapatra, S.S : *Santal Folk Tales (With Oriya Translation) (Bhubaneswar : Academy of Tribal Dialects and Culture, Harijan & Tribal Welfare Department, 1997).*

Man, E.G. : *Sonthalia and the Santhals (Calcutta: George Wyman, 1867).*

Martin, W.B. : *English-Santali Vocabulary (Benaras: Medical Hall Press, 1898).*

Mitra, P. : *Sanhal Vasa (Calcutta: Firma Mukhopadhyay, 1985).*

Mitra, Parimala Chandra : *Santhali: The Base of World Languages (Calcutta: Firma Mukhopadhyay, 1988).*

Mohmmad, L. : *Census of Mayurbhanj State, 1931 (1891; rpt. 1981, Calcuttta: Firma Mukhopadhyay), vol, I, p. 224.*

Mukherjee, C. : *The Santal (Calcutta: Indian Research Society, 1948; rpt. 1962, Calcutta: A Mukherjee & Co.).*

Orans, Martin : *The Santal: A Tribe in Search of Great Traditions (Detroit: Wayne State University Press, 1965), p.106.*

O' Malley, L.S.S. : *Santal Parganas (Bengal District Gazetteers) (Calcutta : The Bengal Secretariat Book Depot. 1910, rpt. 1984, New Delhi : Logos Press).*

Pal, Anadi, : *'Interstilia in Santal Foot', Bulletin of the Anthropological Survey of India, 16 (a & 2), 1967, pp. 41-56.*

Prasad, Onkar : *Santal Music: A Study in Pattern and Processes of Cultural Persistence (New Delhi: Inter-India Publications, 1985).*

Prasad, R. N. & S. Sengupta : *Santal Rural Economy: A Study Based on Village Survey in Santal Parganas (Santiniketan: Agro-Economic Research Centre, 1973).*

Puxley, E. L. (ed) : *A Vocabulary of the Santali Language (London: W.M. Watts, 1868).*

Ray, P. C. : *Socio-Cultural Process and Psychological Adaptation of the Santal (Calcutta: Anthropological Survey of India, 1975).*

Ray T., (comp) : *Santal Rebellion: Documents (Calcutta: Subarnarekha, 1983).*

Ray, Ujjwal, et al (eds) : *To be with Santals (Calcutta: Government of West Bengal, 1982).*

Ray, Chaudhury, Indu: : *Folk-Tales of the Santals (New Delhi: Sterling, 1973).*

Risley, H.H. : *Tribes and Castes of Bengal (Calcutta: Bengal Secretariat Press, 1891; rpt. 1981. Calcutta: Firma Mukhopadhyay). Vol. II, p. 224.*

Roy, S.C. : *'The Aborigines of Chotanagpur', Man in India, 26 (2), 1946, pp. 120-36.*

Roy, Chaudhury, P.C. : *'The Creation of the Santal Parganas' in Bengal Past and Present (Calcutta, 1962).*

Roy, Chaudhury, S.K. : *'ABO Blood Group and haemoglobin Variant in the Central District of Orissa'. Man in India, Sl (3), 1971, pp. 245-51.*

Saha, N.K. : *On Role Analysis: A Study of Inter Personal Relation Among the Santals in a West Bengal village (Calcutta: Prantik, 1972).*

Sarkar, S. S. : *'Blood Group Investigation in India with Special Reference to Santal Parganas, Bihar', Transactions of Bose Research Institute, 12, 1937, pp.89-101.*

Sen, Suchibrata : *Santals of Jungle Mahals (Delhi: Ratna Prakashan, 1984).*

Singh, K. S. : *'Introduction' to Tribal Law and Justice, in A Report on the Santal, by W.G. Archer (New Delhi: Concept Publishing Company, 1984).*

— : *Tribal Society in India: An Anthropohistorical Perspective (Delhi: Manohar Publications, 1985).*

Singh, L. B. : *Santal Youths: An Unseen Talent (New Delhi: Wisdom Publications, 1988).*

Skrefsrud, L. O. : *A Grammar of the Santhal Language (Benares: Medical Hall Press, 1973).*

Thakur, Rudranand : *The Social Matrix of a Tribal Village (New Delhi: Archives Books, 1989).*

Troisi, J. (ed) : *The Santals: Readings in Tribal life (New Delhi: Indian Social Institute, 1979, vols. I-X (mimeo).*

Troisi, J. : *Tribal Religion : Religious Beliefs and Practices Among the Santals (New Delhi : Manohar Publications, 1979).*

Banerjee, Gagan Chandra : *Introduction to the Kharia language (Calcutta: Bengal Secretariat Press 1894).*

Bhattacharjee, P.N. and N. Kumar : *A Blood Group Genetic Survey in the Dudh Kharias of the Ranchi District (Bihar, India)', Human Heridity, 19, 1969, pp. 385-97.*

Karve, I. : *'Anthropometric Measurements in Karnataka and Orissa and a Comparison of the Two Regions with Maharashtra', Journal of the Anthropological Society of Bombay, (NS), 8 (1) 1954, pp. 456-75.*

Prasad, N. : *Land and People of Tribal Bihar (Ranchi: Tribal Research Institute, 1961).*

Raghavaiah, V. : *Tribes of India (Delhi: Bharatiya Adimjati Sevak Sangh, 1972), Vol.II*

Risley, H.H. : *The Tribes and Castes of Bengal (Calcutta: Bengal Secretariat Press, 1891; rpt. 1981, Calcutta: Firma Mukhopadhyay), Vol.I. P.466.*

Roy, S.C. & R.C. Roy : *The Kharias (Ranchi: Man in India Office, 1937).*

Russell, R.V. & Hiralal : *The Tribes and Castes of the Central Provinces of India (London: Macmillan and Company, 1916; rpt. 1975, Delhi: Cosmo Publications), vol. III. P.445.*

Sinha, A.P. : *Religious Life in Tribal India: A Case Study of Dudh Kharia (New*

Delhi: Classical Publications, 1989).

Sinha, D.P. : *The Hill Kharias of Purulia: Impact of Poverty on a Hunting and Gathering Tribe, Memoir No. 59 (Calcutta: Anthropological Survey of India, 1984.*

Vidharthi, L.P. and V.S. Upadhyay. : *The Kharia Then and Now: A comparative Study of Hill Dhelki and Dudh Kharia of the Central Eastern Region of India (new Delhi: Concept Publishing Company, 1980).*

Archer, W. G. : *The Blue Grove: The Poetry of the Uraons (London: George Allen and Unwin, 1940).*

— : *The Dove and the Leopard: More Oraon Poetry (Calcutta: Longmans, Green & Co., 1948).*

Banerjee, P. : *A Comparative Study of Oraon Physical Characters, Calcutta, Bulletin of the Department of Anthropology, Government of India, 9 (2), 1960.*

Bhavani, Enakshi : *Folk and Tribal Designs of India (Bombay: D.B. Taraporevala Sons and Company, 1974).*

Dalton, E. T. : *Descriptive Ethnology of bengal (Calcutta: Government Press,*

1872; rpt. 1960, Calcutta: Indian Studies: Past & Present, Firma K.L. Mukhopadhyay; rpt. 1978, Tribal History of Eastern India, New Delhi: Cosmo Publications).

Das, A. K. and M. K. Raha : *The Oraons of Sundarban (Calcutta: Tribal Welfare Department, West Bengal. 1906).*

Dash Sharma, P. : *'Physical Anthropology of Oraons, Mundas and Dusadhs of Bihar', Journal of the Indian Anthropological Scoiety, 11 (2), 1976, pp. 121-24.*

Dehon, P. : *Religion and Customs of the Uraons (Calcutta: Asiatic Society of Bengal, 1906).*

Elwin, Verrier, : *'An Anthology of Marriage Sermons', Man in India, 23, 1943, p. 108.*

Karve, I. : *'Anthropometric Measurements in Karnataka and Orissa and a Comparison of these Two Regions with Maharashtra' Journal of the Anthropological Society of Bombay (NS), 8 (1), 1954, pp. 45-75.*

Kirk, R.L. et al. : *'A Genetic Study of the Oraons of the Chotanagpur Plateau (Bihar, India)', American Journal of Physical Anthropology, 20, 1962, pp. 375-85.*

Kujur, Alomani Anupa : *The Oraon habitat: A Study in Cultural Geography (Ranchi: Satya Bharati, 1989).*

Kumar, N. et al. : *'Distribution of A1, A2, BO Blood Groups, ABH Secretion in Saliva and the Sickle Cell Trait Among the Oraons of Surguja District, Madhya Pradesh' (Calcutta: Anthropological Survey of India, 1976) (unpublished).*

Lalit, P. Pathak : *'The Enticed Immigrants: Imported Tribal Tea Labourer in Assam, 1941-1960', Journal of Social Sciences and Humanities, (NEHU), 2 (4), 1984.*

Mahalanobis, P. C. et al : *'Anthropometric Study of the United Provinces, 1941: A Statistical Study', Sankhya, 9, 1949, pp. 89-234.*

Mishra, U.C. : *Tribal Paintings and Sculptures (Delhi: B. R. Publishing Corporation, 1989).*

Mukherjee, B. N. et el : *'Serum Protein and Red Cell Enzyme Polymorphism in Oraon Tribe, India' Annals of Human Biology, 2 (1), 1975, pp. 201-4.*

Narayan, Sachindra : *Dimension of Development in Tribal Bihar (New Delhi: Inter-India Publications, 1986).*

Oraon, K. : *The Spectrum of Tribal Religion in Bihar: A Study of Continuity and*

Change Among the Oraon of Chotanagpur (Varanasi: Kishor Vidya Niketan, 1988).

Pandey, Ajit Kumar : *Kinship and Tribal Polity: A Cojparative Study of the Mundas and Oraons of Bihar (Jaipur: Rawat Publications, 1989).*

Piplai, C. et al. : *'A Note on Abo, MN, Rh Blood Groups of the Tamang and Oraon Tea-Labourers of the Jalpaiguri District, West Bengal', Journal of the Indian Anthropological Society, 20, 1985, pp. 66-70.*

Prasad, N. : *Land and People of Tribal Bihar (Ranchi: Bihar Tribal Research Institue, 1961).*

Rath, Govind Chandra: : *Industrialization to indigenization: A Study on Cultural Reformulation of a Tribe in Orissa (Calcutta: Centre for Studies of Social Sciences, 1987).*

Risley, H. H. : *The Tribes and Castes of Bengal (Calcutta: bengal Secretarat Press, 1891; rpt, 1981, Calcutta: Firma Mukhopadhyay), vol. II.*

Roy, S. C. : *The Oraons of Chota Nagpur their History, Economic Life and Social Organization (Ranchi: Author, 1915).*

: *Oraon Religion and Customs (Ranchi): Man in India Office, 1928;*

rpt. 1972)

— : *Oraon Religion and Customs (Delhi: Gyan Publishing house, 1985).*

Russel, R. V. and Hiralal : *The Tribes and Castes of the Central Provinces of India (London: MacMillan and Company, 1916; rpt. 1975, Delhi: Cosmo Publications), Vol. II.*

Saran, A.B. : *Murder and Suicide Among the Munda and the Oraon (Delhi: National Publishing House, 1974).*

Shukla, B. R. K. and D. Tyagi : *'Morphogenetic Comparison of Two Tribal Groups of Ranchi', Indian Journal of Physical Anthroplogy and Human Genetics, 1975, 1, pp. 56-66.*

Singh, K. S. : *Tribal Society in India: An Anthropohistorical Perspective (Delhi: Mahohar Publications, 1985).*

Toppo, Sita : *Dynamics of Educational Development in Tribal India (new Delhi: Classical Publications, 1979, (1983).*

INDEX